RICKY TIMS'
RHAPSODY QUILTS

INSPIRING, AMAZING—CREATE YOUR OWN!

RICKY TIMS

C&T PUBLISHING

Text and Artwork copyright © 2007 Ricky Tims
Artwork copyright © 2007 C&T Publishing, Inc.

PUBLISHER: Amy Marson
EDITORIAL DIRECTOR: Gailen Runge
ACQUISITIONS EDITOR: Jan Grigsby
EDITOR: Liz Aneloski
TECHNICAL EDITORS: Ellen Pahl and Teresa Stroin
COPYEDITOR/PROOFREADER: Wordfirm Inc.
COVER DESIGNER/DESIGN DIRECTOR/BOOK DESIGNER: Kristen Yenche
PRODUCTION COORDINATOR: Kirstie L. Pettersen
ILLUSTRATOR: Kirstie L. Pettersen
QUILT PHOTOGRAPHY: John Bonath, unless otherwise noted.
ADDITIONAL PHOTOGRAPHY: Ricky Tims and Jeff Bilieau
Published by C&T Publishing, Inc., P.O. Box 1456, Lafayette, CA 94549

Library of Congress Cataloging-in-Publication Data
Tims, Ricky.
  Ricky Tims' rhapsody quilts : inspiring, amazing--create your own! / Ricky Tims.
    p. cm.
  ISBN-13: 978-1-57120-456-1 (paper trade : alk. paper)
  ISBN-10: 1-57120-456-3 (paper trade : alk. paper)
  1. Patchwork--Patterns. 2. Strip quilting--Patterns. 3. Quilting. I. Title.

  TT835.T525 2007
  746.46'041--dc22

Printed in China

10 9 8 7 6 5 4 3 2

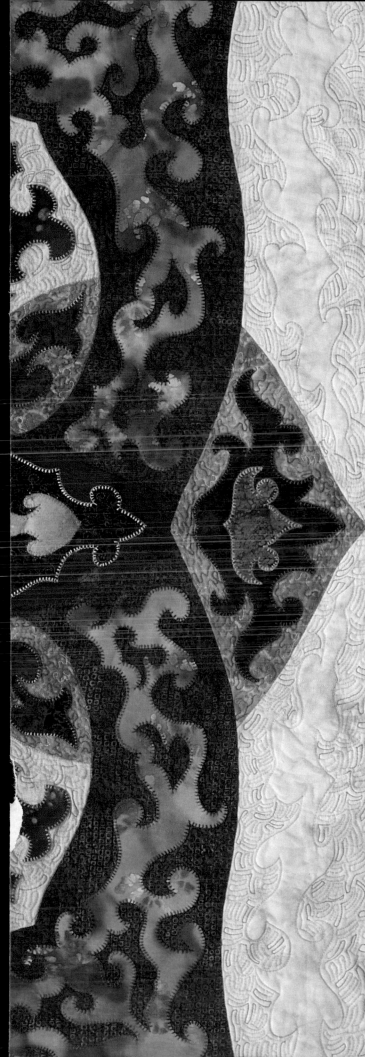

CONTENTS

Dedication

My parents have always given their blessings for my ever-evolving, sometimes crazy and unexplainable endeavors, even when it went against their better judgment. To Mom and Dad, because of you, I keep reaching for the stars.

In recent years, my partner, Justin, has worked tirelessly to help build and manage a complex company that we can realize our personal goals. To Justin, my love is everlasting. I would not have made it this far in my journey without you.

I have life-long friends who have walked with me through life's journey. Good friends are treasures. To these friends, you are always in my heart, and the memories of our friendship help me remember my past.

For the past 16 years, guidance and encouragement have come from casual quilters and quilting professionals alike. To all of you who have influenced me over the years—thank you. I hope I make you proud.

For quilters everywhere who have allowed me to impart a bit of my love, passion, and compassion—not only in regards to quilting, but about the wonderful mystery of life—this book is for you.

May we all believe in the unbelievable and reach for the impossible.

Acknowledgments

Creating a book is not accomplished single-handedly. The book starts with a vision and the publisher must embrace that vision.

Amy Marson saw my vision and enabled this project to move forward at lightning speed.

Darra Williamson worked diligently to make sense of my hen scratches and organized this text into a logical and well-organized progression of ideas.

Liz Aneloski's creative genius has assembled all of the ingredients together and presented it with beauty and style.

The entire creative and technical staff at C&T Publishing is responsible for taking my vision and making it a reality.

The efforts of all these people on my behalf have enabled this book to be an amazing reality. Thank you all.

INTRODUCTION

I love quilting. I love quilters. I love teaching and sharing my passion with anyone who will listen. I love seeing the expressions on the faces of visitors to Tims Art Quilt Studio and Gallery who walk in and ask, "Where are the quilts?" expecting to see work that is more reminiscent of their childhood recollections. It's great providing an education to those who think quilting is still in the dark ages.

I don't love the quilt police. I don't enjoy seeing students oppressed by limitations put upon them by some "quilt authority" who made laws regarding the quilting process. Quilting should be fun. It should be rewarding. It should not be stressful. If you like rules and boundaries—that's okay. If you want freedom of expression—that's okay too! I like to say, "Whatever pickles your okra!"

I have fun with my quilting. It is fun to teach and see the "lightbulb" moments in students. I guess if it ever stops being fun, then it is time to move on to something else. I've had a lot of obsessions in my life, but quilting is the addiction that has stuck with me the longest.

Those who know me know I really have fun with it all. I make "serious" quilts, but I'm not serious about making them. It is important to learn what needs fussing over and what does not. This book is a guidebook, and while it is a how-to book, it is not a book of rules (even if I use the word). It outlines the methods I use, but nowhere do I intend to imply that *my* way is the *right* way. Again—whatever pickles your okra!

I'd like to think that I could be witty and whimsical throughout this book, but the fact of the matter is, there is a lot of information and some of it requires some reasonable amount of concentration by you, so I won't muddle it up with quips and cleverness. I hope you'll appreciate that. If you want to see the whimsical side of me, I invite you to attend one of my two-day seminars around the country or one of my weeklong quilt retreats in Colorado.

However, not wanting to deprive those of you who would like a joke, here goes:

One day there was a thread that was working hard in his garden under the hot sun. Being tired and a bit distracted, he got tangled up in the weed-eater. Once he pulled himself from the weed-eater, although not entirely back to normal, he decided to take a break and go to the local bar to throw back a cool one. When he entered the bar, the bartender bristled, looked at the thread and said, "Hey, we don't serve your kind. You're a thread." The thread just looked at him and said, "No, I'm afraid not!"

Now, on to more serious matters . . .

I guess, given my lifelong love for and involvement with music, and the fact that many of my quilt titles have musical references, it is not surprising that I am writing a book about a style of quilt I call a Rhapsody quilt. I've come to realize that there are many similarities between one of these quilts and a musical rhapsody. Each unfolds like a mystery—with twists and turns that move in unexpected directions. A musical rhapsody and a Rhapsody quilt both have a thoughtful, overall "structure," and yet within each there remains a great deal of flexibility that tends only to be realized as the work evolves. Like a musical rhapsody, a Rhapsody quilt can include a variety of themes and motifs, played out in flowing patchwork and intricate appliqué. Even so, the overall design maintains focus and unity.

Sometimes forces we do not recognize, know, or understand motivate our most creative choices. Recently I was presenting a seminar on Rhapsody quilts. After one session, a student came up to me and handed me a piece of paper that explained the origin of the word *rhapsody*. It is derived from the Greek words *rhaps*, meaning "to sew," and *ÿodieï*, meaning "a song." In other words, the literal translation of the word rhapsody is "to sew a song." Was this a collision of art and music fate, coincidence, divine intervention, and serendipity at work? I couldn't say, but I can't image a more perfect way to describe these beautiful quilts . . . and once again, blend my two passions.

Throughout my quilting experience, I have found that new techniques take a bit of practice before I become confident and proficient with them. There are many techniques in this book that are a bit out of the ordinary and will likely be new to you. The techniques are not difficult, but like anything new, you'll need a bit of practice to learn the process. My advice is to read through the directions first, and then make samples following the directions for each. Once you are confident, you will not be fearful when working on your masterpiece.

It's time to begin your own unexpected journey composing your own beautiful, quilted song. This book will provide all the guidance you need to create your own, one-of-a-kind, twenty-first century legacy quilt—a Rhapsody quilt!

SONGE D'AUTOMNE, 82″ × 82″
Completed in 2000. Machine pieced, machine appliquéd, and machine quilted with trapunto by Ricky Tims.

The design for this quilt began with straight lines and had been planned with Amish colors. At the last minute, I made the lines wavy and used original 100% cotton hand-dyed fabrics.

This quilt was the immediate predecessor to my Rhapsody quilts. The similarities include symmetrical layout (although not mirrored), curved piecing, and set-in corners. The medallion-style design with appliqué on the main areas is also reminiscent of a Rhapsody quilt. It relates to other Rhapsody quilts in that it was created by making improvisational choices on a fixed background design.

This quilt was completed on the first day of 2000—a true new-millennium quilt. It won the Master Award for Machine Workmanship at the 2000 International Quilt Association Show in Houston, Texas. From the collection of the International Quilt Festival—Houston and Chicago.

WHAT IS A RHAPSODY QUILT?

A Rhapsody quilt is a medallion-style quilt that utilizes a symmetrical design in a reversed and mirror-imaged arrangement. The design is usually—although not necessarily—composed of gentle curves (see *Rhapsody in Green* on page 36). The basic "skeleton"—or outline—of the quilt offers opportunity for original appliqué or lush quilting. Although the quilt has a symmetrically organized layout, the addition of appliqué or other details can be more spontaneous.

Although I had experimented with the various elements utilized in subsequent Rhapsody designs, *Bohemian Rhapsody* (page 9) was the first quilt to bring all these elements together and it was the first quilt to incorporate the designation "rhapsody" in its title. It is a significant quilt in the fact that it established the Rhapsody quilt's signature style, even though at the time I had no idea that the formula or process would be something I would repeat—much less put in a book.

What exactly is that signature style?

Rhapsody quilts are all about symmetry. The design is reversed and mirror-imaged over a central vertical and horizontal axis. In most cases, there are no seams along the axis lines.

Rhapsody quilts are typically square due to the method used to create them. While it *is* possible to create a rectangular Rhapsody quilt, this book will focus on designing and making square quilts.

Rhapsody quilts almost always feature appliqué. As with most appliquéd quilts, the appliqué is applied to the background blocks before the blocks are joined together. However, in a Rhapsody quilt, the "blocks" are oddly shaped background units as opposed to the typical square blocks associated with a traditional appliqué quilt.

An appliquéd Rhapsody "block." Note the odd-shaped piece filled with appliqué.

BOHEMIAN RHAPSODY, 86″ × 86″
Completed in 2002, machine pieced, machine appliquéd, and machine quilted by Ricky Tims.

This quilt began as a small, original, paper-cut-style medallion block. The symmetrical undulations are loosely based on a traditional Diamond-in-a-Square motif. The urns and other appliquéd motifs create large, circular effects.

Bohemian Rhapsody is made from original 100% hand-dyed cotton fabrics, and I used silk and rayon threads for the machine quilting. Creating the quilt was very improvisational—so much so that I ended up replacing the original medallion from which the quilt emerged. The hard work paid off. Not only did I have a quilt that I loved, but it also won five Best of Show awards and numerous other prizes, including the blue ribbon for Innovative Appliqué—Large at the 2002 International Quilt Association Show, held in conjunction with Quilt Festival in Houston, Texas, each fall.

Even now, with the format well defined, I let each Rhapsody quilt evolve. I encourage you to do the same. This is an *improvisational process*. At various times along the way, sit back with a cup of your favorite beverage, and look at how your quilt is progressing. Let the quilt have a voice, making suggestions about color, fabric, and the shape of an appliqué. The only fixed aspect of the design is the shape of the templates used for the background pieces. Everything else remains fluid until you stitch it or fuse it down—and sometimes even *that* is flexible. Continue, as you work, to stir and simmer, to add "salt and pepper to taste." Listen to your inner voice. This is not a quilt you will make in a weekend . . . or a week. It may take months—or more—to produce a Rhapsody quilt. You are, in essence, creating a legacy quilt, a quilt that will likely become a family heirloom. Give it—and yourself—the attention and the patience it deserves.

By following the guidelines in these pages, you can create your own original design and make a stunning quilt—one that appears much more complicated than it really is.

My dad is a quilter. He and I both began quilting in 1991. His first quilt was a king-size Broken Star with hundreds of diamonds. It is a family treasure, but it did have its problems. So in 2002, with improved skills, Dad wanted to make another star quilt. He pieced the entire star and I added the setting, appliqué, and quilting.

This quilt, while incorporating a traditional Lone Star motif, still meets the criteria for a Rhapsody quilt. It has a reversed and mirrored design centered on a vertical and horizontal axis. If you notice the size of this quilt and understand that standard fabric widths do not allow for a quilt this large to be made using the corner techniques described in this book (page 19), you will wonder how I did it. The secret here is that I created miters in the border corners and used appliqué to cover most of the seam, so the seam is hardly noticeable.

DAD'S LONE STAR, 82″ × 82″
Completed in 2002, machine pieced by Richard Tims and Ricky Tims.
Machine appliquéd and machine quilted with trapunto by Ricky Tims.

RHAPSODY TECHNIQUE
AT A GLANCE

Rhapsody quilts are all about symmetry. The design is reversed and mirror-imaged over a central vertical and horizontal axis. Rhapsody quilts are typically square and almost always feature appliqué. In a Rhapsody quilt, the "blocks" are oddly shaped background units as opposed to the typical square blocks associated with a traditional appliqué quilt.

This chapter is an overview of the steps to create a Rhapsody quilt. It is an introduction to and brief summary of the process. For additional details, refer to the pages indicated in each section.

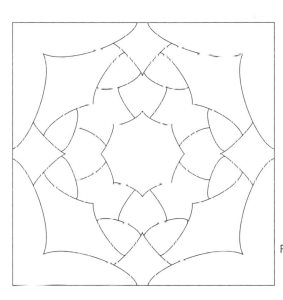

Rhapsody design

CREATE THE SKELETON
For additional details, refer to pages 24–29.

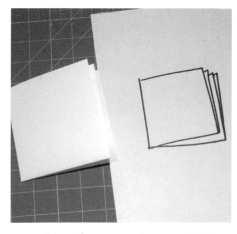

Fold an 8½˝ square of paper in half horizontally and then vertically.

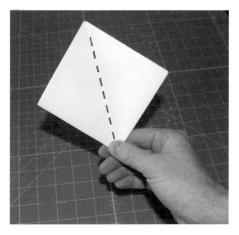

Hold the square with the cut edges at the top and the folds on the bottom; make a vertical, diagonal fold.

Using a pencil, draw a curved line to represent the border. Unfold the paper to check the border design.

Once you are satisfied with the border line, refold the paper and draw other divisions to create "blocks" for the skeleton of a potential Rhapsody quilt.

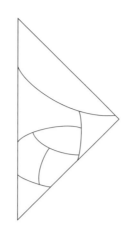

Design for a skeleton created by drawing a series of curved lines.

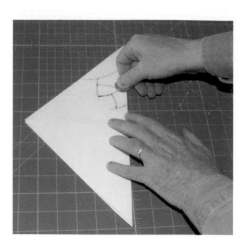

Unfold the paper, then refold diagonally. Rub with a coin to transfer the design.

Darken the transferred lines.

Repeat to transfer the ¼ image, open the paper, and darken the lines.

Transfer the ½ image, open the paper, and darken the lines.

CREATE A FULL-SIZE PATTERN

For additional details, refer to pages 30–33.

Cut a large, perfectly square piece of freezer paper to ¼ the finished size of the entire quilt, piecing it as needed. Fold it in half diagonally. Sketch the design, or project it on the wall. Trace it onto the dull side of the freezer paper and add registration marks.

Refold the freezer paper, transfer the drawn lines, and darken the lines to create the ¼ design.

PREPARE THE MASTER TEMPLATE

For additional details, refer to page 34.

Cut away the parts of the design that touch the horizontal axis. Butt their edges together with the corresponding parts on the vertical axis; tape them together to make templates.

Cut out the center template, which is ¼ of the design.

Trace the center template to make 4 pieces and tape them together. This makes a complete set of full-size master templates.

PREPARE THE UNITS FOR SEWING

For additional details, refer to pages 38–41. The templates shown in these photographs are those used in the practice exercise to learn curved piecing.

Iron the cut-out freezer paper templates to the right side of your chosen fabrics and roughly cut out around the edges.

Stay stitch around the template and add the registration marks in the seam allowance.

Trim the seam allowance to a scant ¼˝, remove the paper, and place the fabric on a design wall.

THE APPLIQUÉ

For additional details, refer to pages 42–46, and 47–57.

Create your appliqué designs and draw them on the pattern templates.

Prepare and fuse the appliqué pieces onto the background pieces.

Note: This photo shows a practice design for appliqué stitching.

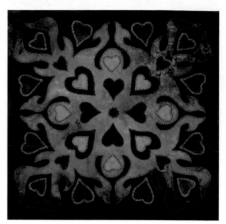

Stitch around the appliqués using a machine blanket stitch.

SEW THE PIECES TOGETHER

For additional details, refer to pages 57–68.

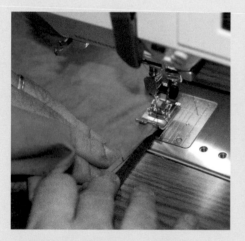

Sew the background pieces together aligning the stay stitching and registration marks.

Continue sewing, straightening the curves as you sew and matching the registration marks. Sew all of the background pieces together to complete the quilt top.

This photo shows a completed pieced rectangle used as a practice design for sewing curved seams.

RHAPSODY
QUILT DESIGN

he background of a Rhapsody quilt consists of large areas of unusually shaped pieced units. The process of creating these unique and unusual shapes begins with a drawing. I call this drawing the "skeleton" of the design. The skeleton is used to create full-size templates; once created, it is the least flexible element of the quilt. All other parts of the design can be continually changed or revised as you go along.

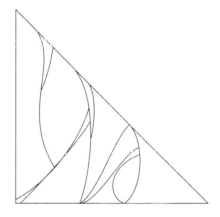

This triangular drawing represents ⅛ of the *Bohemian Rhapsody* design.

Read through the following pages before you begin to experiment with creating skeletons. You'll find some good, solid information to help you with basic design, as well as design information as it applies specifically to the Rhapsody quilt format.

The skeleton for *Bohemian Rhapsody*

DESIGN FROM THE OUTSIDE IN—
The Number One Design Rule for Creating Patchwork

In my classes on design, I give the class a quick assignment: Draw a traditional Log Cabin block. No ruler, no measuring—ready, set, go, just sketch the block. I give them about a minute to do this. Give it a try. I'll bet that just like over 90% of the class, you'll attempt to draw the block the way it is constructed: from the inside out. The sketch *looks* like a Log Cabin block, but it is likely rather crude.

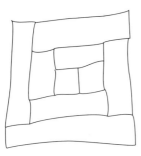

Draw a Log Cabin block.

Listen up, now. Here's a valuable lesson: The best and most logical way to create a patchwork design is to draw it from the *outside in*, not the *inside out*. In other words, draw it in the *reverse* order from the order in which you will piece it. I call this the "Number One Design Rule for Creating Patchwork."

Any two-dimensional design starts with a "canvas." In quiltmaking, the canvas is contained within the outer edges of the block or the quilt. In the case of the Log Cabin block, the canvas *is* the block.

Now try drawing the block again, only this time, establish the canvas first. Draw the outline of the block. Now draw a "slice" from left edge to right edge. The slice represents an area that I call the "forbidden zone" ("out of bounds" to you sports fans). It is the last "log" of the block as it is sewn, but it is the first one to be drawn. The rest of the block is an "active area," open and available for additional lines.

Forbidden zone

Draw the outline of the block, then a line from edge to edge.

Draw another slice (or log), beginning at the line of the previously blocked-off forbidden zone and continuing to the edge of the canvas. Now there are two parts to the forbidden zone. The rest of the area is still active and available for dissecting.

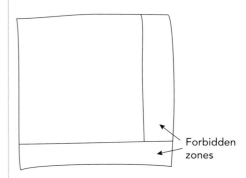

Forbidden zones

Draw another line. Now there are two forbidden zones.

If you continue to cut slices in this manner, eventually you will end up with the Log Cabin block. I suspect you'll find, as my students inevitably do, that in comparing the two sketches, the second sketch—even drawn freehand—looks much more refined.

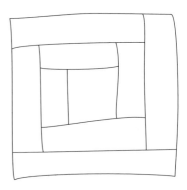

Continue drawing lines to make a Log Cabin block. Even freely drawn, the block looks more refined.

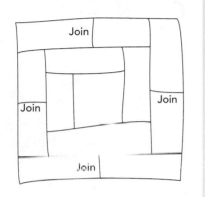
This simple principle—designing from the outside in—gives you the freedom to create just about *any* patchwork design you can imagine— even designs with curves! You'll want to remember this rule when you are creating your Rhapsody design.

DESIGN NOTES FOR RHAPSODY QUILTS

Let me start out by saying that there is often a tendency to "see" things in your skeleton design, like tulips or body parts, for example. (Don't laugh! I've had it happen in class many times.) Once you've seen them, it is hard to ignore them. You'll see them every time you look at the skeleton and want to change the design.

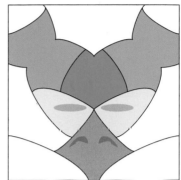

Like a tulip . . . or a yellow-eyed monster!

I can reassure you, however, that these phantom images will not be obvious once they become backgrounds for appliqué. When you look at the bare skeleton, your eye focuses on lines. The finished quilt will have color shapes filled with appliqué and the focus will change. If you create a drawing that causes you to focus on an odd shape, chances are it won't look that way in the finished quilt. No one else will notice, but you'll always get your laugh. If you truly can't stand it, change it now or make another skeleton!

The monster has disappeared.

Design Ideas

These are designs I hope to make someday, although I already have more designs than I'll ever complete in my lifetime.

This is one of many Rhapsody designs I have created that is still only on paper.

This design, tentatively called *Rhapsody Christmas*, will present some very interesting and complex construction problems. However, I plan to meet the challenge. The templates for this quilt are ready to go.

How did I create these designs? I drew the lines on the skeleton triangle as you will learn in Creating the Skeleton (page 24). Then I added squiggles to represent appliqué bits inside the areas. Using a computer program,

I copied and pasted the design to give me a representation of how the quilt would "fill out" with appliqué (see Designing With a Computer on page 20). It's not necessary to do this with a computer; I just enjoy playing with the possibilities. I'm sure I won't create appliqué identical to this, but it gives me an idea of how the finished quilt will look.

Take away the appliqué and you'll see that the skeleton is really quite minimal. It proves that the drawing in the original triangle can be fairly simple, but the resulting quilt can end up looking very complex.

The triangle for the skeleton of *Rhapsody Christmas*

The most complicated pieced design I have done is this *Sunflower Rhapsody* (page 19), which will have appliqué only in the four large corners. This is the quilt currently in progress on my design wall. The center is complete; I'm still in the process of appliquéing the sunflowers in the corners; then it will be time to quilt.

I don't recommend creating this much complex piecing. Unless you are confident in your piecing ability. Here is a photo of the quilt in progress.

This *Sunflower Rhapsody* quilt is all pieced, except for the four corners with small sunflower appliqués. As of this writing, the quilt is nearing completion. It is about 72˝ square.

 Tip

If you like your overall drawing, but feel a particular section needs refining or adjusting, you can erase and redraw that section, but you'll need to erase and retrace matching lines in all the remaining sections to see what your design will ultimately look like.

How Fabric Dictates Size

When you are designing your quilt, the L-shaped corner/border templates in a Rhapsody quilt can be quite large. If you use my No-Pins Set-In Corners technique (page 58), the quilt will not have a seam at the corners like a quilt made with a traditional butted or mitered border. Instead, the corners will most likely be created from *curved* L-shaped templates that can really eat up the fabric.

The piecing secret to a Rhapsody quilt is hidden in the centers of the top and bottom, and left and right sides. There needs to be a seam going *off the edge* at those points. If you have designed your quilt with four L-shaped border pieces, these seams will come together and touch in the middle of the quilt's edges, and the width of the fabric will limit the size of your finished quilt.

Fabric off the bolt tends to measure about 42˝ wide to 44˝ wide at most. Therefore, you can't have a border piece wider than 44˝, including the seam allowance. For quilts that have side seams that touch, the corner template must not be larger than 43˝. (A safer size would be 42˝.) Because this measurement represents ½ of the quilt, the largest Rhapsody quilt you could make would be 84˝ square.

These borders do not have corner seams, so the width of the fabric will restrict the size of the finished quilt.

There *is* a solution. If you design a border with an additional template separating the corner L shapes, as shown below, you can stretch the design to make a larger quilt. I wouldn't do this, however, unless the end result creates a pleasing overall design.

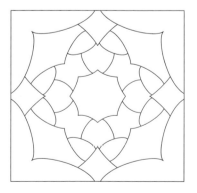

This design has a template that slightly separates the L-shaped borders. This added feature allows for a slightly larger quilt.

DESIGNING WITH A COMPUTER

I like to draw by hand. It is fast and an eraser is a quick fix. However, I also enjoy using the computer to create and experiment with various Rhapsody designs. I almost always use paper and pencil to make the original drawing on my triangular "canvas," but then I take a photo or scan it into my computer and use a drawing or photo program to manipulate it into a complete, virtual Rhapsody design.

You don't need to be a computer expert to make a Rhapsody design. The computer simply provides the opportunity for quickly creating a reversed and mirrored design.

If you want to try creating your skeleton on the computer, upload a photo of your triangular drawing or scan it into the computer. Once you open it in a drawing program, you can crop the triangle, then flip and mirror it to create your skeleton without using the tracing method described on page 26.

If you are comfortable and competent with drawing and graphic design programs, you can even do your revising and coloring without ever picking up a pencil and paper!

DESIGNS OUT OF CONTROL— AVOIDING THE PITFALLS

Not every Rhapsody design you create will be a success. (Ask me how I know this!) Some of you may be able to transform the skeleton into something fabulous with just a few simple changes. With others, it's better just to start over again from "square one." This is why I advocate trying a variety of designs right from the start so you'll have several to choose from.

Here are some examples of designs with problems . . . and potential solutions.

The first design is very simple, but it is begging for appliqué. Notice that the center seams at the top, bottom, and sides run off the edges. This is very characteristic of a Rhapsody quilt and there are not really any technical problems with this simple design.

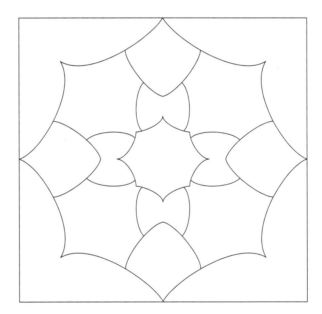

Simple, effective design needs appliqué.

The first problem with the design is that there are no seams going off the edges, so the entire border is one template—and one fabric. It also has intricate curves that would be complicated to piece, and I would suggest simplifying it. The four small, diagonal "pointed peanut" shapes near the center would be possible to sew, but if these lines represent sewing lines (as the lines of a skeleton are meant to do), then this would be fairly difficult to recreate with piecing. The same is true for the deep curves near the top, bottom, and sides of the quilt.

These elements might, however, be appliquéd, so give your design some thought in terms of alternative construction methods before you give it a final thumbs up or thumbs down.

Border has no seams; piecing is difficult.

This design is really nice; well balanced and visually pleasing. However, it is basically appliqué upon appliqué. (If you were to try and piece it, the seams would need to be set-in, and set-in, then set-in some more.) This design ignores the principles of the Number One Design Rule for Patchwork. It is just shapes on top of shapes.

Nice, but for appliqué only.

Here is an example of a skeleton that got out of hand. There is too much going on and it doesn't leave much room for appliqué. The lines are crisscrossed and disorganized. The borders, if any, are weak; they don't "hug" the quilt.

Too complicated and borders are weak.

While the design on page 22 is not complicated, there are many areas that could be problematic. Neither the outermost border nor the next border has a seam anywhere. It would be possible to piece these, but with fabrics limited in width to 44", the size of this quilt would be dictated by fabric width. Adding units in these open borders would allow for a larger quilt and make the piecing easier. The center would be difficult to piece, although it could be appliquéd.

Border has no seams and piecing would be difficult.

By adding just a few seams, the border problems can be solved, but I'd still recommend adding seams to the center for easier construction.

Borders can now be pieced, but center is still difficult.

The first design below is an example of a design that is not contained. It has potential, but really needs a border. Instead of starting over, you could simply add a border as described in Borders: Give Your Quilt a Hug (page 26) and erase any lines that extend into the new border area. The modified design that follows is much better.

This design is not bad, but seems a bit uncontained with the seams flying off the edges.

The same design has been modified to include a border that hugs the design.

Here's another example of a design and how it evolved. You can try the final design yourself; it is included in Designs to Try (Skeleton 1, page 72).

Using the principal of dividing or dissecting the canvas from the outside in, the lines on this triangle were drawn in the order shown.

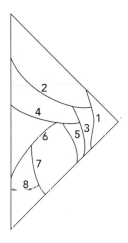

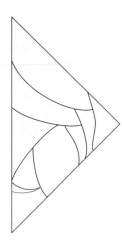

One line modified

Once the design was transferred to make ¼ of the skeleton, I could tell immediately that I wouldn't like the center. It needed a bit more curve and I thought bringing line 8 to form a point at the fold would make the design look better.

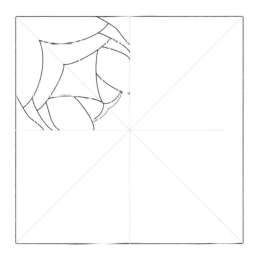

The center is more pleasing.

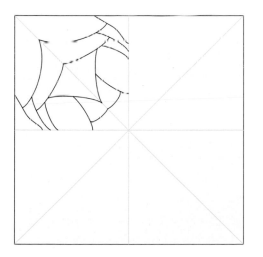

Center of design was not pleasing.

So, I made the change shown in red. Once that small change was made, the design became more pleasing. Ultimately, it is a personal choice, but I like the second version better.

The complete, final design

YOUR RHAPSODY QUILT

The first stage of designing your Rhapsody quilt is to create the design for the background. Do this by drawing what I call the skeleton, which is used to create full-size templates. To draw the skeleton, you will fold a square paper to create a small triangular area; consider this your "canvas." You will add lines to the triangular canvas that represent the pieced seams in your quilt background. These lines will be repeated to create reversed and mirrored elements that will become the all-important skeleton of your quilt. Once established, you should think of the skeleton as being the one static and unchangeable element of your design. Altering it after the process is possible, but can be dicey. (More on that later.)

I recommend that you draw several skeletons before deciding on one for your project, and be sure that you understand the principles of Design From the Outside In (page 16) before you begin.

CREATING THE SKELETON

⬥ WHAT YOU'LL NEED

A regular pencil: You know the kind—the old-fashioned pencil with a #2 lead that you can sharpen. You need to press down hard to make very dark lines when you draw. The graphite in a mechanical pencil is usually too delicate.

8½″ squares of paper: Cut these either from 8½″ × 11″ printer paper or from freezer paper. I like freezer paper because it is a bit more transparent. (As you read through the instructions for constructing a Rhapsody quilt, you'll quickly discover that I'm a freezer paper nut!) Prepare several sheets of paper.

A coin or other hard, blunt tool, such as a Popsicle stick or plastic spoon: Use this to help transfer your drawn designs.

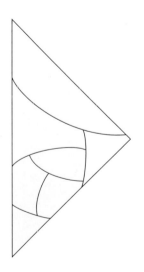

Triangular "canvas" with piecing lines

Folding the Paper

1. Fold an 8½″ square of paper in half horizontally and then vertically as shown to make a folded square. (I work in this size because it is easy to use, easy to scan, and easy to make multiple copies on a copy machine for experimenting with color and other options.) If you are using freezer paper, fold it with the shiny side in.

Fold the paper in half horizontally and vertically.

2. The last fold is the most critical. There are two diagonals on which to make this final fold. One works, the other doesn't. To make the correct diagonal fold, hold the folded square in your hand on point (like a fan), so that all the cut edges are at the top and all the folds are on the bottom.

Hold the square with the cut edges at the top and the folds on the bottom.

3. Now, imagine a line running north to south (top to bottom). Fold the paper on this imaginary line by bringing the left point over to touch the right point. Now you have a triangle positioned with the longest side on the left, all cut edges on the top diagonal, and all folds on the bottom diagonal. This will make eight divisions; the final triangle is ⅛ of the total design.

Correct

Incorrect

Drawing the Design: Keep It Simple

It is easy to make your skeleton too complicated. Consider this: The background of an exquisite Baltimore Album quilt can be just a bunch of plain white blocks. The detail and excitement are in the appliqué and quilting. The same is true for your finished Rhapsody quilt. Its main dazzle is in the appliqué and quilting; the background should be simple.

In a Rhapsody quilt, the skeleton outlines the unusual shapes I refer to here as blocks. Keep the skeleton clean and basic. A few lines in your triangle canvas will create enough interest for the background. Trust me on that!

Borders: Give Your Quilt a Hug

Rhapsody quilts are most successful when the border is incorporated into the design right from the outset. When you fold the paper to make the all-important ⅛ triangle, train yourself to recognize which edge represents the outside edge of the quilt. If you look at your folded triangle, it would be the short side of the triangle without any folds. Then *draw your border first*. Draw it so that it is "heavy" and embracing. I find there is a tendency for most students to create a wonderful outline—or skeleton—but with an undersized (too narrow) or wimpy border—or even no border at all! Remember that the border is the final "hug" for the design—and nobody likes a wimpy hug, so be sure to give this aspect of your design plenty of focus and weight.

When I design my skeleton, I start with the border. Remember the Number One Design Rule for Creating Patchwork? If the border is the first line you draw on your skeleton, it will be the last seam you sew when you assemble the quilt.

Draw the first curved line from the top of the folded edge (longest edge) to the opposite short edge. This is your "border" line. Unfold the paper and take a peek. You'll need to imagine the mirror image, or you can lightly trace the line to the opposite triangle to see how the border will look. Once you feel good about your border design, read on and have fun randomly drawing the lines for the remaining structure of the quilt.

Draw the first line to represent the border.

When opened and mirrored, the narrow point in the corner results in a border that will be too wimpy.

Alter the border and make it more pleasing.

Refold the paper into a triangle and draw other division lines to create the skeleton.

Other Design Lines

1. Draw a series of curved lines on the top side of the folded paper. Keep the curves gentle and flowing, working from the outside in, and use your pencil to divide your triangular canvas into sections, going from edge to edge or by connecting lines. Avoid drawing a specific "shape," as these are more difficult to piece and are better candidates for appliqués. Darken the lines heavily. We don't want any wimpy lines here! The sample below is intended as a reference only; I encourage you to draw your own original variation. Refer to Design Notes for Rhapsody Quilts (page 17) for guidance . . . and for pitfalls to avoid.

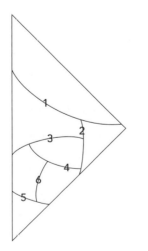

These numbers represent the order that the lines were drawn.

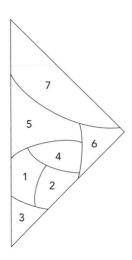

This is the piecing order; but note that this is only ⅛ of the design.

2. Unfold the paper to the original 8½″ square and then refold the paper diagonally in one direction, with the drawn section inside, as shown.

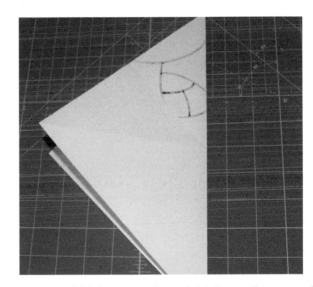

Unfold the paper, then refold diagonally.

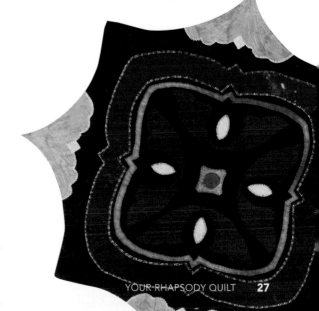

3. Place the folded paper on a hard, flat surface, with the drawn portion (facing inside) on the top. By orienting the drawn portion on top, it is visible through the paper without a light table. Using a coin, Popsicle stick, or other hard, blunt tool, apply sufficient pressure to rub directly on the lines of the drawing you created. (I mean, really "scrub" it!) The graphite from the pencil inside the fold will transfer the mirror image of the design lightly onto the paper opposite the diagonal fold. I call this a "ghost tracing." I do this exercise with hundreds of quilters at a time in a large auditorium and they manage easily, even with regular printer paper. However, if the paper is especially dense, you may find it necessary to transfer the design using a light box or by placing the paper against a bright window.

Rub to transfer the design.

4. Open the paper and darken the faint lines of the newly made ghost tracing. You've completed ¼ of the design.

Darken the lines.

5. Fold the paper in half, right sides together, along either the vertical or horizontal axis. Use the coin or blunt tool to transfer the ¼ image to the opposite quadrant of the folded paper to create a ghost tracing. Open the paper and darken the newly traced lines. Half of the design is now complete. (I bet you can see where this is going!)

Transfer the ¼ image, open the paper, and darken the lines.

6. Refold the paper in half, so that the completed half is face to face with the blank half of the paper. Use the coin or blunt tool to transfer the entire half of the design to the opposite side. Open the paper and darken the lines of the ghost tracing to complete the skeleton of your design.

Transfer the half image, open the paper, and darken the lines.

7. The piecing order for this skeleton is the opposite of the way it was drawn. First join all 1 and 2 pieces in a ring. Set in piece 3. Add the remaining pieces in numerical order as shown.

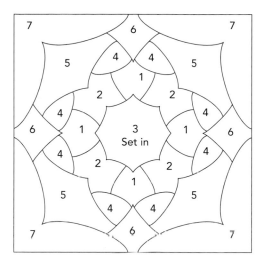

Piecing order

 Tip

I enjoy making several sample designs before making the final decision for the skeleton of my quilt. I learn a lot about how the basic design will work and the experiments give me a variety of options from which to choose. Remember: A Rhapsody quilt is not a quilt that you will complete in a weekend. This is an heirloom, a legacy quilt. Why not spend a few extra hours now to find the absolute best design for *your* personal legacy?

UNDERSTANDING THE DESIGN

The overall design you have created is essentially four equal quarters separated by a horizontal and vertical axis. When you remove ¾ of the design, the horizontal axis and the vertical axis are located on two sides of the remaining portion of the design. Now, any template that falls on or touches the horizontal axis will have a counterpart, or mate, on the vertical axis. However, in most cases, although the design is created this way, once you begin sewing the quilt together, there will be no pieced seams in the fabric along either axis. How can that be?

When you transfer the design to make templates, you will transfer only ¼ of the full-size design onto freezer paper. While it *is* possible to consider the axis edge as a fold line when cutting the fabric as you do in garment sewing, it won't work for the precise piecing methods included in this book. I prefer to cut and reassemble the existing pattern, combining the half or partial templates into one; this makes accurate templates and eliminates vertical and horizontal seams.

Isolate and study the upper left ¼ section of the design you have drawn. The vertical axis is on the right edge of this section and the horizontal axis is on the bottom edge of this section.

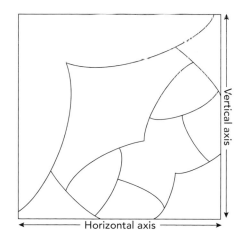

Vertical axis

Horizontal axis

In the diagram below, the arrows indicate the "movement" of two of the horizontal-axis templates. They will be repositioned, butted to their counterparts on the vertical axis, and taped together to form a single piece. All templates falling on edges of the axis will eventually be joined in this manner, including the center of your design. You will make a joined template for that, too.

¼ of the design in the original skeleton

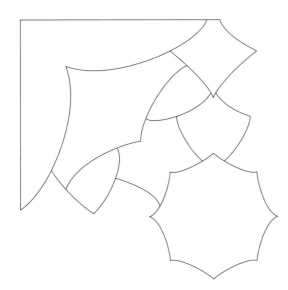

The design looks like this when the templates have been cut away, repositioned, and joined to their counterparts.

Once you understand these concepts, you are ready to enlarge your design and begin making full-size templates.

CREATING A FULL-SIZE PATTERN

By now you have probably figured out that you do not need to make full-size templates for *each piece* in the quilt design. Because the design is reversed and mirrored, ¼ of the design will provide templates for the entire quilt. (This includes a template for the center of the quilt. More on that later.) The first step is to enlarge the necessary portion of the final design to full size by extracting it from the 8½˝ piece of paper and transferring it to a large sheet of freezer paper.

◆ WHAT YOU'LL NEED

Freezer paper: You will need to piece together freezer paper to create a *perfectly square* piece on which to draw ¼ of your full-size Rhapsody design. The size of the quilt you wish to make will determine the size of the square. You will use the freezer paper design to make the templates.

A regular pencil: Use a #2 pencil, the kind you used to create the skeleton.

Transparent tape

Ruler or yardstick

T-square or right-angle (90°) triangle ruler

Different-colored pencil: This is to make easily identified registration marks.

For the Close is Good Enough method of enlargement (page 31), you will also need:

A coin or other hard, blunt tool, such as a Popsicle stick or plastic spoon: You'll use this to help transfer your drawn designs.

For the Accurate Transfer method of enlargement (page 32), you will also need:

A copy machine

An overhead projector or other, similar piece of projection equipment

Transparent plastic sheets for overhead projectors

At this point, you must decide how large you want the finished quilt to be, if you haven't already. Remember that the width of your fabric will limit the size of your quilt (see page 19). Quilting will undoubtedly cause your quilt to shrink up a bit, so plan your quilt top to include an extra 1″ to 2″, —the larger the quilt, the more potential for shrinkage. So, for example, if you want the finished quilt to measure 80″ square after quilting, plan a quilt top that is about 82″ square. Divide the width of the quilt top in half, which is 41″ in our example. Therefore, you would need a 41″ square of freezer paper for the Rhapsody design.

Most freezer paper comes on an 18″-wide roll. Tape appropriate lengths of paper together, on the dull (paper) side, with long strips of transparent tape until the width of the paper is sufficient for your project. Butt (don't overlap) the edges of the paper and tape every inch of the seam. Do not place any tape on the shiny side. Trim the top, bottom, and side edges as needed to make an accurate square.

I can't stress enough how important it is that this piece of freezer paper be perfectly square. If the paper is not square, the templates will be off, and the pieces will not fit together. Use a ruler to make sure the sides are all the same measurement and a T-square, the corner of a right-angle (90°) triangle ruler, or some other squaring device to make sure the corners are a true 90° angle. Have someone else double, or even triple, check your square.

> ### ◆ SIZE FORMULA
> Determine the size you want for your finished quilt. Add 1″ to 2″ to allow for shrinking when the piece is quilted. Divide this number by 2. This equals the size of the paper square you'll need for enlarging the design and creating templates.

Enlarging the Design

I have two methods for enlarging the design. The first doesn't require any equipment beyond a regular #2 pencil. The second requires an overhead projector or another, similar piece of projection equipment. Both options are effective, so read through the two methods and decide which one is most appropriate for you.

The "Close is Good Enough" Method

1. Refold your 8½″ drawing to the original ⅛ triangle.

2. Fold the large freezer paper square diagonally once, with the dull (paper) side out. The tiny folded triangle and the large diagonally folded triangle now each represent ⅛ of the total quilt. Compare the orientation of the small drawing and the large, diagonally folded piece of freezer paper. The diagonal fold of each should be oriented the same way.

3. Use a regular #2 pencil to freely sketch the design from the small drawing onto the large piece of freezer paper. Compare sides and proportions of the 2 drawings and adjust the large drawing as necessary. I made a crease in the center of the triangle as a reference point to help me sketch the lines. You can do this or not, as you choose. Just make sure your lines are graceful and flowing. Bumpy lines will make bumpy seams later. Once you are satisfied with the large drawing, darken the lines with pencil.

Fold in half diagonally and sketch the design.

4. Using a different colored pencil, make ¾″- to 1″-long, clearly visible registration marks at random intervals 1½″ to 2″ apart along each line of the large drawing. Note that I used a red permanent marker for better visibility in the photograph. Be sure to use a colored pencil so that the marks will transfer.

Add registration marks to the sketched design.

5. Open the large piece of freezer paper and refold it along the same diagonal fold, this time with dull (paper) sides together. Place the folded paper on a hard, flat surface, with the drawing as the top layer. Using a coin or another hard, blunt tool, apply sufficient pressure to rub on the lines of the drawing you created to make a ghost tracing. Press on the registration marks to transfer them as well. Open the paper and darken the lines and registration marks.

Transfer the drawn lines and registration marks.

The Accurate Transfer Method

This method requires the use of a projection device. No excuses, now! You may not have one, but I'll bet you know someone who does: a neighbor, your church, your office, or the library. Remember: You are making a quilt that your progeny will probably fight for when you are gone—an album quilt of the twenty-first century—so borrow a projector if necessary. You'll only need it for about 30 minutes. Someone is bound to be willing to help you.

1. Use a copy machine to make a transparency of your complete 8½″ drawing. Use transparent plastic sheets that are designed for use in overhead projectors.

2. Fold the large freezer-paper square diagonally once with the dull (paper) side out and secure it to the wall with the fold at a 45° angle and the other edges perfectly vertical and horizontal.

Fold the freezer paper diagonally and secure to the wall.

3. Using an overhead projector, adjust the image so the projected ⅛ image is accurately positioned on the corresponding triangular section of the large piece of freezer paper. Use a regular #2 pencil to trace the projected design onto the freezer paper; darken the lines if necessary to make sure you will get a good transfer. Use a different-colored pencil to make clearly visible registration marks ¾″ to 1″ long, at intervals 1½″ to 2″ apart along each line of the large drawing.

Trace the design and make registration marks.

4. Remove the drawing from the wall. Open it, and refold it along the same diagonal fold, this time with dull (paper) sides together. Place the folded paper on a hard, flat surface, having the triangle with the drawing as the top layer. Using a coin or other hard, blunt tool, apply sufficient pressure to rub on the lines of the drawing to make a ghost tracing. Be sure to transfer the registration marks as well. Open the paper and darken the lines and registration marks.

ALTERNATE PROJECTION METHODS

■ Scan the original 8½″ drawing into your computer. Transfer the design to the large sheet of freezer paper using an LCD projector and the Accurate Transfer Method.

■ If you have a digital camera, photograph and download your original ⅛ folded triangle design instead of scanning it. Project the digital photo and transfer it, following Steps 2 through 4 for an accurate enlargement of the design.

■ Take a slide of your original ⅛ folded triangle design and use a slide projector to project the enlarged image onto the paper.

PREPARING THE MASTER TEMPLATE

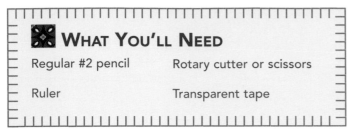

What You'll Need

Regular #2 pencil	Rotary cutter or scissors
Ruler	Transparent tape

1. Once you have the ¼ design drawn full size on freezer paper and all registration marks are in place, add lines parallel to the horizontal or vertical axis to indicate the straight grain on each template. Working with one template at a time, use scissors or a rotary cutter to cut away each template that touches only the horizontal axis. Cut exactly on the drawn lines. I use a rotary cutter to cut my templates, but you may prefer a good, sharp pair of scissors.

Cut away each template touching the horizontal axis.

2. Move the cut-out template so that it is next to its matching counterpart, or mate, on the vertical axis. Butt the edges together and tape the two templates together along the entire butted edge, creating a single template from the two. The new template will be a symmetrical, mirror-image template.

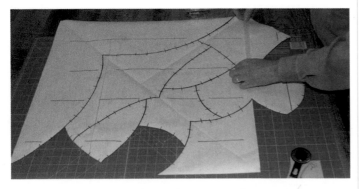

Butt the edges and tape the two templates together.

3. Cut the center ¼ template from the master template on the marked lines.

Cut out the center ¼ template.

As with other shapes on the master template, the area that incorporates the center of the design is only a portion of the actual unit, the center being ¼ of the actual design. Trace the ¼ pattern and create three additional, identical templates. Tape them together on the horizontal/vertical axis edges to make the complete shape with all the registration marks you need to join the seams.

Tape the four center templates together.

WORKING ON A DESIGN WALL

As I mentioned earlier, making a Rhapsody quilt is a very improvisational—and also lengthy—process. It involves lots of thought, experimentation, and what I call "fiddling and futzing" along the way. In other words, this is not a quilt you want to design on your living room floor! The quilt is also built one template at a time, from the center out. (It's designed from the outside in, but pieced from the center out. I can't imagine making a Rhapsody quilt without my trusty design wall.

Creating a suitable design wall is neither difficult nor expensive. If storage is a problem, don't worry: I've got that covered too.

Building a Design Wall

You'll want the surface of your design wall to be at least as large as the quilt you have planned. Here's what I suggest:

Go to your favorite home or building supply store and purchase two sheets of 1"-thick Styrofoam wall insulation. This material is very lightweight and typically comes in 4' × 8' sheets, so two sheets should do the trick. When you get home, butt the sheets together along their long edges and hinge them by running a long strip of tape (I love duct tape!) down the front at the join. If necessary, you can trim the Styrofoam to reduce the size of your design surface. Cover the surface with a large piece of white or off-white needle-punched 100% cotton batting, such as Warm & Natural (see Resources on page 92). Carefully pull the excess batting over the edges of the wall and secure the batting to the back with pins, tacks, staples, or tape.

The hinge allows you to fold the wall and store it, when not in use, behind a door or under the bed.

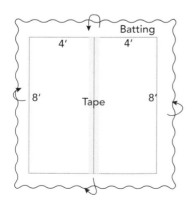

Make a design wall.

Selecting Fabrics

I recommend that you don't make all of your fabric decisions before starting a Rhapsody project. This is an exercise in improvisation, and you'll want to take everything one step at a time and let the quilt unfold each step of the way.

My key piece of advice is this: Start with a palette of colors you like. Include a range of values (light, medium, and dark) to provide contrast and to enable the design to pop. Don't be afraid to use bold colors, but ultimately choose colors that *you* like. The characteristic symmetry of the typical Rhapsody design often enables you to consider unusual color combinations.

I recommend that you use 100% cotton fabrics. I dye my own fabrics; these one-of-a-kind fabrics help create the distinctive look of my quilts (see Resources on page 92). I have to admit, I've fallen in love with the particular fabric I use for dyeing because it creates a luxurious suede look in the finished quilt. But you don't need to use hand-dyed fabrics to make a successful Rhapsody quilt.

What about prints? This is a tricky question. I think that the design of a Rhapsody quilt comes from the background skeleton and the appliqué, and I feel medium-to large-scale prints would compete for attention with these key elements. However, I'm also a firm believer that you can make a Rhapsody quilt using fabric that I might not consider, as long as you give it careful consideration and it ultimately works for you. See *Arabesque* on page 76 by Daphne Greig for an example of a wonderful quilt made with textured prints. Any good-quality quilting fabric will work, as long as you choose fabric you like. The most important thing is to be yourself and use whatever fabric pops your buttons!

RHAPSODY IN GREEN, 58″ × 58″
Completed in 2004, machine pieced, machine appliquéd, and machine quilted by
Ricky Tims. Original, 100%-cotton fabrics hand-dyed by Ricky Tims and Justin Shults.

This quilt is a good example of how unusual colors will blend and complement each other when they are organized using the design formula outlined in this book. From the collection of Barbara and Bob Hunter.

Most traditional album-style quilts have a light background, with appliqués cut from darker, contrasting fabrics stitched on the blocks. While there are examples where the background is the darker fabric, these tend to be the exception and not the rule.

However, in a Rhapsody quilt, the background is neither light nor dark, but a combination of both, creating a contrast in value that delineates the various shapes and provides a lot of visual interest. While I know there are always exceptions, the background of a Rhapsody quilt is best limited to only three to five fabrics. If you look at the examples in this book, you'll see the interaction of the background colors and notice that only a few fabrics are used in any one quilt. *Bohemian Rhapsody,* for example, includes four background colors: red, navy blue, lavender, and a bit of orange. Other colors are introduced in the appliqué fabrics.

The appliqué fabrics may be limited as well, but this will ultimately depend on your appliqué designs (see Designing the Appliqué on page 42). The most obvious choices for appliqués will be fabrics that contrast with the background—that is, a light value on a dark value or a dark on light. However, I use an appliqué technique called Outline Appliqué (page 50) that highlights, rather than hides, the stitches. With this method, two fabrics (the background and the appliqué) that are similar in color or value can still be distinct if I use a contrasting thread on the edge of the appliqué. So, in essence, I am able to introduce yet another color with the stitching. This is not essential; it's just something I enjoy doing, something indicative of my personal style.

Bohemian Rhapsody: Note the four background colors: red, navy blue, lavender, and orange.

 Tip

Make several copies of your original (8½″ square) skeleton. Shade the areas with different gray values from light to dark. Value is more critical than color. If you like, you can color in the shapes on another copy to get an idea of the colors you might like. Even though there have been times that I've colored my small design, I've never used the colors from my drawing. The quilt seems to request its own choice of colors. All I have to do is listen.

NO-PINS PRECISION CURVED PIECING

No-Pins Precision Curved Piecing is the perfect solution when you need to sew seams for designs with medium- or large-scale templates that have unusual shapes and curved edges (hmmm . . . sounds like a Rhapsody quilt). It is the method I prefer, to achieve maximum precision when I am joining curved seams. This method utilizes stay stitching and registration marks. When the final seams are sewn to join the pieces, the registration marks are matched and the stay stitching is lost in the seam allowance.

Preparing the Units

To practice this technique, use a freezer paper rectangle that measures 8″ × 12″. Draw a curved line on the dull side, similar to the one shown below and add registration marks. For this practice piece, use the straight sides of the rectangle as your straight grain lines. Cut the rectangle apart along the curved line. Then follow the steps below to prepare a background piece using the No-Pins Precision Curved Piecing method.

Draw a curved line.

1. Iron each template, shiny side down, onto the right side of the chosen fabric, matching the grain lines. Rough cut the fabric about ½″ away from the edge of the freezer paper.

Tip

When using freezer paper templates that are pieced together, avoid pressing over the transparent tape whenever possible.

2. Use a regular stitch length to stay stitch the fabric *just barely* beyond the perimeter of the template. This stitching may be a single-stitch width beyond the perimeter, ¹⁄₁₆″ beyond the perimeter, or any similar tiny measurement. When I do my stay stitching, I like to see a gap about a needle's width between the edge of the paper and the stay stitching. Whatever miniescule distance you choose, it should be consistent. It is *your* official "special distance." Train your eye to recognize this measurement. We'll be referring to it a lot in the future.

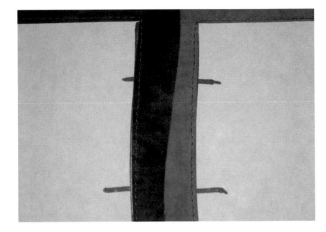

Stay stitch your special distance from the edge of the template.

The purpose of this stitching is to identify the seam line (represented by the edge of the template) once you have removed the freezer-paper template, just before the units are joined. If the stay stitching is too far from the template, you'll be left with a guessing game when it is time to piece, and precision will suffer. If the stitching is too close to the template, it will be difficult to sew the seams without the stay stitches showing on the quilt top. Learning the proper distance will take a bit of practice.

3. Once you have stay stitched around the edge of the templates, use a distinctive marking tool to transfer the registration marks onto the fabric (between the stay stitching and the edge of the fabric), so the markings are clearly and easily visible in what will be the seam allowances. (Often a regular #2 pencil is sufficient.)

Do not mark in the narrow special distance between the edge of the freezer-paper template and the stay stitching. You want the markings to be well hidden in the seam allowance after the seams are sewn.

These registration marks are vital! You will use them for aligning your pieces on the design wall, but more important, they are the most critical elements on your "block" when it comes time for you to piece your units together. For this reason, make sure they will be easily visible three years from now. (Hey, I know you! You are just like me and it might take that long before some of you are ready to piece. <Grin>)

Registration marks

4. Trim the excess fabric to slightly less than ¼" from the edge of the template, *not* the stay stitching. (Again, I use a rotary cutter, but use scissors if you prefer.) An exact seam allowance is not required, and it is much easier to sew curves with a seam allowance that is just slightly smaller than ¼".

Trim seam allowance.

5. Remove the freezer-paper template and place it on the design wall to keep it handy and ready to be used for the next ¼ of the design. You will use each template 8 times (4 times to cut the background pieces and 4 times to mark the appliqué designs onto each background piece).

6. Place the prepared fabric piece on your design wall. If you plan to add appliqué, you *can* add it now, although I find it helpful to prepare all the background pieces before I add any appliqué. This allows me to evaluate the background for the entire quilt and to make any changes before tackling the appliqué.

7. For the practice exercise, turn to Sewing the Pieces Together on page 57 to sew the pieces of the rectangle together.

Piece by Piece: Build Your Quilt on the Wall

Do not cut your full-size master template apart into individual templates all at once. Instead, beginning from the center, cut and prepare one template and fabric piece at a time.

WHAT YOU'LL NEED

Your master template	Transparent tape
Regular #2 pencil	Fabric
Ruler	Design wall
Rotary cutter or scissors	

1. Check to make sure you have drawn lines to indicate the direction of the grain line on each shape of the master template.

2. Cut the center template from your master pattern and prepare the center fabric piece as described in Preparing the Units (page 38). Position the prepared center piece on your design wall, in the center, taking care to place the horizontal/vertical axes properly. Use the paper template, the registration marks, and the grain line of the fabric to help you determine the correct placement on the design wall.

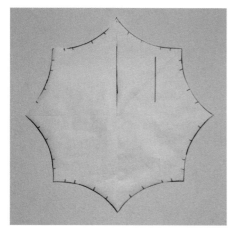

Correct positioning

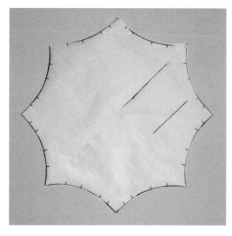

Incorrect positioning

The prepared fabric from the center template
in place on the design wall

Note

Do *not* attempt to fold the fabric into quarters and use the ¼ template to cut the center area. I'm always trying to find shortcuts and ways to beat the system too, but this particular trick does not allow for the precision necessary to successfully piece a Rhapsody quilt.

3. Working from the center out, use the next template—one that touches the center unit—to prepare the next fabric piece. Repeat the steps of ironing the freezer paper template to the fabric, stay stitching, transferring the registration marks, and trimming the seam allowance for each unit, and continue building the body (or background) of the design on the design wall. In most cases, the last pieces to go in place will be the outermost borders that you drew first in the design.

Prepare and position the pieces working
in a logical progression from the center out.

All the background pieces prepared and positioned on the design wall

In *Bohemian Rhapsody* (page 9), 8 lavender, football-shaped pieces circle around the center medallion. I first envisioned these background areas as bright yellow; in fact, this area of the quilt sat in bright yellow fabric on my design wall for many days before I replaced the shapes with the perfect lime green. Hmmm. That stayed for a while until I realized, no, that won't work either, so I tried the lavender. I don't know how else to describe it other than to say it just *felt* better. I let my intuition guide me.

As I continued putting background pieces on my design wall, I realized that the lavender needed to reach out and repeat itself in other places of the design, but in small pieces, not big chunks. So I took my big, chunky templates and sliced into them. I altered my large background pieces to the perfect size of the trimmed large template, and I used the trimmed bit as a template for extra lavender. These lavender bits were not part of the original skeleton, but by making a change along the way, the design finally worked.

Tip

Can you make changes to a template? The answer is yes, but you must be careful to make them only to the interior. You can take a template, add a line representing a seam, cut on that line and turn that template into two templates. Doing this subdivides the template and divides a forbidden zone as previously described (page 17). When it is time to piece together the quilt, you'll need to sew those pieces together first before you can join it to the next piece. If you look at *Bohemian Rhapsody* (page 9), you'll see that there are lavender slivers separating the red and navy fabrics. These were changes I made to the original template. I added them to provide a bit more interest, but I didn't do it until very late in the process.

Study your color choices as you go. Follow your intuition. If a particular color or value is not working, try substituting a different fabric. You should be pleased with the overall appearance of the background structure before beginning the appliqué stitching. You may want to jump the gun and try exploring appliqué designs, and that's okay. But obviously, the background will set the stage for the entire quilt.

Tip

Freezer-paper templates have a tendency to curl once they have been cut. To remedy this, briefly press the template, shiny (waxed) side down, on your ironing surface. Peel the pressed template from the surface and it will be much flatter and more manageable.

DESIGNING THE APPLIQUÉ

The truth is, you can plan the appliqué and where it will go pretty much at any stage in the design of a Rhapsody quilt. Just make sure you plan and stitch the appliqués before you begin to piece the background shapes together. Keep in mind that the smaller background units are much easier to maneuver for appliqué than the entire quilt top, so you'll want the appliqués stitched before the quilt is assembled. And for another reason—and this is always a biggie for me—you never know when you might want to change a fabric, a color, or even an appliqué shape.

Sources of Inspiration

Inspiration for appliqué designs abound. All you need to do is look around you. For example, Rhapsody quilts make the ideal canvas for creating a travel memory. Quilters are notorious for taking photos when they travel, intending them as inspiration for future quilts. But, as we all know, very often these photos remain just photos.

You can give these images a showcase by adapting them as appliqué designs for your Rhapsody quilt. You'll probably need to tweak the image some, but the results can be stunning.

A while back, I took a photo of iron grillwork on the old Federal Building and Post Office in downtown Pueblo, Colorado. The dragons on that ironwork became the inspiration for my quilt *Fire Dragon Rhapsody* (page 43).

Detail of dragon appliqué on *Fire Dragon Rhapsody.* I didn't copy or trace the photo; not because it would have been inappropriate or illegal—those designs are in the public domain—but because as they were, they wouldn't "fit" the background templates.

Why not go through your collection of photos—digital or otherwise? I bet you'll find a wealth of inspiration there. In addition to your own personal photos, there are lots of sources (books and the Internet) of copyright-free designs for you to adapt into appliqués. Better yet, you can create your own original designs. It's easier than you think. You'll read more about this later.

I've presented Rhapsody design classes to quilters who do not come from art backgrounds and who don't think they can draw. At the end of the class, we are all always thrilled (and sometimes amazed) with the results of their attempts. So don't tell me you can't do it. That's an excuse I cannot accept. I believe you can. It may take time—and revising, drawing and erasing, and revising again—but you can do it *if you believe you can.* Some of the quilts selected for this book were made by doubters—and look what they accomplished! (See the Gallery of Quilts beginning on page 74.)

Grillwork on the Federal Building and Post Office in Pueblo, CO—inspiration for my *Fire Dragon Rhapsody*

FIRE DRAGON RHAPSODY, 62″ × 62″
Completed in 2004, designed, machine pieced, machine appliquéd,
and machine quilted with trapunto by Ricky Tims.

The inspiration for this quilt came from photographs I took of the iron grillwork on the windows of the historic Federal Building and Post Office in Pueblo, CO. Justin Shults dyed the fabrics.

This design utilizes more intricate patchwork and quilting and less appliqué than other Rhapsody quilts. It won the award for Best Machine Workmanship at the 2006 American Quilter's Society Show and Contest in Paducah, KY and is in the permanent collection of the Museum of the American Quilter's Society.

Creating the Appliqué Designs

As with much of the design for a Rhapsody quilt, the process of creating and placing appliqués is all about "give and take." Once you get the background pieces up on your design wall, live with the design a bit. My first thought for *Bohemian Rhapsody* (page 9) was to leave the large, red triangular background areas completely open to show off lots of lush and fancy quilting, but the more I lived with the in-progress design, the more the quilt seemed to say, "Put appliqué on me, put appliqué on me." It took a little while, but eventually I listened. Sometimes that's all you need to do: Stand back for a while and listen to what the quilt has to say. I've discovered that the quilt is very often right.

Detail of appliqué on *Bohemian Rhapsody*. The quilt said, "Appliqué me here," and I listened.

Decide which templates will have appliqué and which will remain open and available for quilting. Take your time, listening to the quilt as you go along.

Considering Size and Scale

The appliqué design should fill the background space. There's nothing lonelier than a wimpy appliqué swimming in a big, wide-open background.

Even though the motif shown below tries to emulate the shape of the background, it is too small to fill the space and will look out of proportion in the finished quilt.

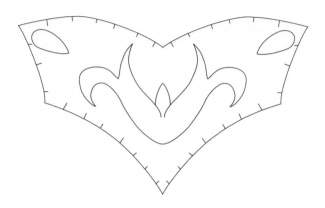

Appliqué design is too small.

It makes sense, then, that to fill the background space, the appliqué must fill the full-size template. Remember: the template does not include the seam allowance, so the edge of the freezer paper represents the sewing line. Don't hesitate to create appliqué designs that come within $\frac{1}{2}$", or even $\frac{1}{4}$", of the edge of the template.

This mirror-imaged design fills the template nicely, and in typical Rhapsody quilt style.

Appliqué design fills the space.

Besides filling the space, the appliqué should be graceful. If you notice that the appliqué designs, or certain areas of it, are oversized or "chunky," alter them. An easy way to alter a chunky appliqué is to take "bites" out of it. The appliqué design below looks chunky and unfinished.

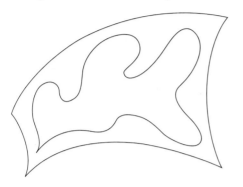

Appliqué design is too chunky.

No need to start over. Just make some alterations. The blue lines added in the version below just cut (or bite) into the design that was already there. One blue line has gone beyond the original appliqué, and extending lines or curves of a design can work well to help fill space.

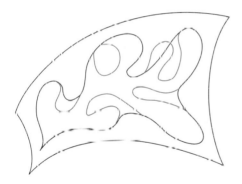

Modify the design.

With a few simple erasures, you can see how different the design has become. This still needs some tweaking, but it is appliqué-friendly and not nearly as chunky as the original.

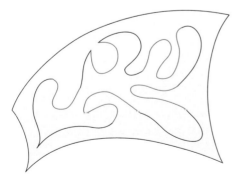

Modified design

To Mirror Image . . . or Not

You can echo the symmetrical design of your quilt's background by creating mirror-image appliqué motifs to fill the background spaces, as you can see in the detail of *Rhapsody in Green* below. Of course, a true mirror-image appliqué motif will only fit a background shape that is itself a symmetrical shape.

Detail of *Rhapsody in Green*. Note the mirror-image appliqué and how nicely it fills the background shape.

To create a mirror-image motif, you can sketch a design on ½ of the dull (paper) side of the appropriate freezer-paper template (use the master template, or make a duplicate, if you prefer). Fold the template in ½ and transfer the ghost tracing to the other ½ of the template, using the same method you used to create the original template (page 28).

The dove motif (page 46) is a good example of an appliqué design that is not a mirror image. You can certainly use non-mirror-image or nonsymmetrical appliqué designs in your Rhapsody quilt; in fact, sometimes these are the only type of design that fits the space. In reality, the dove appliqué would be rather fat and chunky because the illustration is very small and the background template would be quite large. If this happens to you, your intuition will kick in and tell you that the shape is too large for a single appliqué. You won't know this until you begin drawing your design actual size on the templates, though.

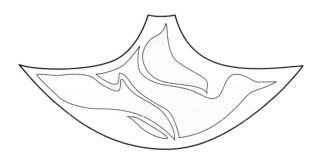

Dove motif is not a mirror image.

To make the dove design less bulky, add appliquéd details on top of the larger appliqué, or create areas of reverse appliqué to break up the chunky, "cookie-cutter" look. This provides more visual interest and creates a more pleasing, refined design.

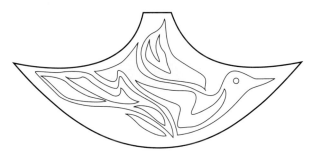

Modified dove

To create a reversed and mirrored center design for your quilt, use the template for the center and the same method of folding and tracing that you used to make the skeleton—creating something more like a paper snowflake or Hawaiian appliqué.

Fold the center template into ⅛ and draw a design.

Mirror and transfer the design to the entire center template.

You can also consider a nonmirrored motif for the center, such as a vase or still life—or a dragon, as I did for the centerpiece of *Fire Dragon Rhapsody* (page 43)—as the focal point of your quilt. That is the fun—letting the design evolve into your own unique Rhapsody creation.

Marking Your Appliqué Designs

Use a regular #2 pencil to draw full-size appliqué motifs directly on the dull side of the appropriate freezer-paper template (that you set aside), and keep a good eraser handy for any modifications.

If you feel awkward about marking up your master template, simply trace the template onto another piece of paper—yes, I use freezer paper—and work on a duplicate template. You want the appliqué design to fit the template and emulate its shape.

Once you are 100% comfortable with your appliqué design decisions, you are ready to begin the appliqué process. Read through the appliqué instructions in the next chapter. Have fun playing with fabrics and always keep your options open. I tend to wait until I have the entire design (background pieces and appliqué motifs) on my design wall before I begin doing anything permanent, such as fusing or stitching. The designs and fabric choices may change several times before I settle on a final version.

SEWING TECHNIQUES
FOR RHAPSODY QUILTS

The following pages walk you step by step through a variety of specific sewing techniques that I use to construct my Rhapsody quilts. I suggest you read through this chapter carefully and make a test sample of each technique so you feel comfortable with the stitching before you begin assembling your own legacy quilt.

MACHINE APPLIQUÉ TECHNIQUES—FEAR NOT THE "A" WORD

Dare I mention the "A" word, lest some of ye scatter to the four winds while others of ye leap for joy? Appliqué! Okay, there! I've said it.

I remember my first attempts at appliqué. As a matter of fact, you can see these glorious efforts on my first quilt (ouch!) and the tree on *Timeless* (page 48—ouch, ouch!) made during my first few months as a quilter. I realized very early on that appliqué was *not* going to be my thing, so for years I avoided it.

My first quilt, made in 1991. Don't laugh too hard—we all have to start somewhere!

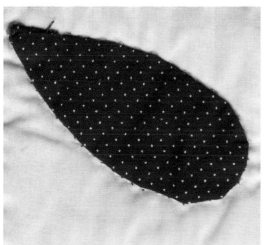

Detail of the appliquéd Honey Bee block from my first quilt

TIMELESS, made in 1991.

Then Suzanne Marshall, renowned for her hand appliqué, shared with me some of her hand appliqué techniques, and I practiced them on *Fandance* (page 49). That entire quilt grew from the center panel, which was originally intended as a practice piece. The rest of the quilt is pieced. Back then I preferred exploring innovative piecing techniques and rarely used appliqué on my quilts.

FANDANCE, made in 1992.

Somewhere along the way, however, I realized that I was limiting my design options by not including appliqué. In more recent years, I've started including appliqué in many of my quilts. I have come to realize that appliqué fosters spontaneity and allows for a more improvisational approach to a design.

Naturally there are as many techniques for creating appliqué as there are books on the subject. In the following pages, I share a style of appliqué that has become unique to my own Rhapsody quilts. This doesn't mean you must do your appliqué my way. I encourage you to use whatever method you enjoy and with which you are comfortable—including hand appliqué and reverse appliqué.

As I developed as a quilter, I found myself drawn to machine techniques. I love the look of hand appliqué, but I prefer to work by machine. The method I use is distinctive and fun. It is a refined method of raw-edge appliqué that I call Outline Appliqué.

Tip

Some people ask whether the block will shrink upon stitching the appliqué. I don't find that to be the case. I use a stabilizer called Ricky Tims' Stable Stuff (see Resources on page 92) that keeps things pretty secure when I machine appliqué. I realize that quilters who hand appliqué sometimes have this problem. If you choose to hand appliqué, I would recommend rough cutting the fabric about 1″ larger than the template all around. Use a temporary marking method to outline the template on the fabric, and then stitch the appliqué inside those boundaries. After the appliqué is stitched, remove the temporary marking and iron the freezer-paper template for that unit in place over the appliqué. Proceed to add the stay stitching and registration marks as described on page 38. This should eliminate the issue of distorted blocks or shrinkage due to hand stitching.

Preparing for Outline Appliqué

I have used the Outline Appliqué technique on several quilts. It is a raw-edge appliqué technique that utilizes fusible interfacing and machine blanket stitch. In most cases, I enjoy incorporating trapunto underneath the appliqué for a more sculpted look. The key characteristic of Outline Appliqué is that rather than trying to disguise or hide the stitches, the stitching becomes an integral design feature that accentuates the appliquéd elements. I demonstrate my trapunto techniques on the *Ricky Tims Presents Grand Finale: Fine Machine Quilting and Finishing Techniques* DVD (see Resources on page 92).

Please practice the Outline Appliqué technique before stitching on your Rhapsody quilt. I've provided a pattern called *Rhapsody Hearts*; it will create a 12″ block to use for practice.

Rhapsody Hearts

Rhapsody Hearts block (pattern provided on page 71)

Note: Rhapsody quilts utilize freezer-paper for templates because the template must be ironed to fabric when the background units are prepared. The same freezer-paper templates are then used for drawing the appliqué designs. For this practice sample, you don't have to use freezer paper, but it helps reinforce the technique if you do.

When you are designing a Rhapsody quilt on your design wall, *do not* fuse any appliqués until you are completely confident that you are satisfied with the design and fabric choices. Steam-a-Seam2 is sticky prior to fusing and enables you to position your appliqué elements and leave them for weeks if necessary, giving you the option to make design changes without having to redo everything!

1. Cut a 12″ square of paper. Fold in half horizontally and vertically. Trace the *Rhapsody Hearts* pattern (page 71) matching the center of the paper with the center of the pattern. Trace the pattern 4 times to make the complete design. I like to trace it onto the dull (paper) side of a 12″ square of freezer paper, which is more transparent than printer paper. You don't have to use freezer paper; do whatever greases your skillet.

2. Place the square of main appliqué fabric wrong side up on your ironing surface. Remove the protective paper from one side of your Steam-a-Seam2 and place the fusible sticky side down on your main appliqué fabric. (The protective paper that remains on the other side of the fusible will be facing you.) Smooth the fabric and the fusible web to remove any pleats or puckers and make sure the fusible does not extend beyond the edges of the fabric or it will adhere to your ironing surface. Trim the fusible if necessary.

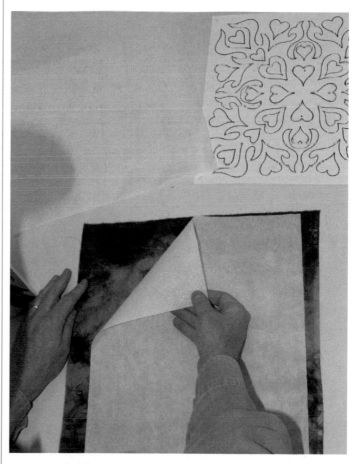

Place the fusible, paper side up, onto the fabric.

3. Use a hot iron to quickly press the fusible web to the wrong side of the fabric. It will only take 2–3 seconds to heat the fusible and adhere it to the fabric—but not permanently, yet. Allow the paper and the fabric to cool.

Press.

4. Carefully peel back a portion of the protective paper backing. The fusible should stick to the fabric, but if the fusible clings to the paper instead, reposition the paper and apply the iron again for 2 or 3 more seconds.

5. With the protective paper peeled back but not removed, place the pattern you created in Step 1 onto the sticky fusible, aligning the design with the grain of the fabric.

Peel away the paper backing and place the pattern.

6. Bring the protective paper back into place over the pattern. Use a regular #2 pencil to trace the design onto the protective paper. (The protective paper is *very* transparent at this point, so this will be easy to do without a light table or window.) Trace the entire design, both the main appliqué and the accent pieces, so that you can use it as a placement guide for the accent pieces later. The pattern on page 71 is color coded so you will know which is which.

Replace the paper over the design and trace.

7. Once again, peel away the protective paper and carefully remove the original pattern. Reposition the protective paper back onto the sticky fusible web and press quickly to secure it to back onto the fusible web. Do not apply the iron for more than a few seconds. You are not trying to fuse anything yet—your goal is just to re-adhere the protective paper back to the fusible web.

Peel away the paper backing and remove the pattern.

8. Cut out the design, through all layers, right on the traced lines.

Cut out the design.

9. Fold the 13″ background fabric square in half vertically and then horizontally; fingerpress lightly along the folds. Open the background square and place it right side up on your ironing surface. Remove the protective paper completely from the main appliqué piece (Step 8) and center the fabric, fusible side down, on the background square. Make sure the appliqué is properly oriented and that the straight of grain is aligned on both pieces.

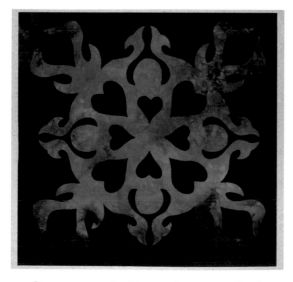

Remove paper backing, and center appliqué on the background square.

10. Once you are satisfied with the placement, use a hot, dry iron to fuse the main appliqué to the background. This should take 7–10 seconds, but I suggest you refer to the manufacturer's instructions for specific details (pressing time and heat settings) for the product you are using.

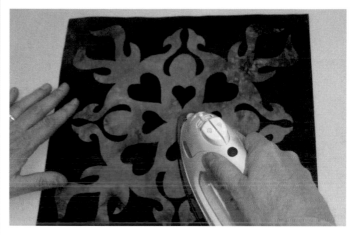

Fuse in place.

11. Trace the heart and circle patterns and prepare the accent pieces using the same procedure. Fuse the accent pieces to the block.

Prepare and fuse the accent pieces.

❁**Tip**

If you have trouble positioning the accent pieces, place them approximately where you think they should be. Place the protective paper left from cutting out the main piece over the block. By using the drawing as a reference, you can easily nudge the accent pieces into position.

Stitching the Appliqué

I prefer to use a contrasting thread color to outline the appliqués, and to provide highlights and texture to the finished piece. My choice of thread varies from project to project. Sometimes I prefer rayon threads, but on other occasions I choose silk or polyester. *Bohemian Rhapsody* (page 9) took 10,000 yards of red silk thread for the appliqué and quilting. The double blanket stitch, which I use frequently, makes any thread appear heavier. The weight of the thread will alter the results. Always, *always, ALWAYS* (got that?) make test samples on the fabric and stabilizer you plan to use to finalize your thread choices—or not, if building the barn twice is your idea of fun.

The Blanket and Double Blanket Stitch

The blanket stitch is a common option on many sewing machines. The double blanket stitch is not offered as a standard stitch on all machines.

Machines vary in the way they create the blanket stitch. However, they all have horizontal (side) stitches and vertical (forward and back) stitches. The diagrams show the individual stitches of the single and double blanket stitches typical on many models of Bernina sewing machines. For clarity, the diagrams show the double blanket stitches side by side, but when actually sewn, the stitches fall directly on top of each other, creating a heavier, thicker-looking stitch. Your machine's stitches may vary, but the most important thing to learn is the stitch pattern of your machine, so you know where you are in the pattern and can pivot the appliqué without having a stitch jump into an unexpected area.

Single blanket stitch

Double blanket stitch

Varying the stitch length and width yields different results. Most often, I use a setting of 2mm wide and 2mm long, but sometimes I prefer a 1.8mm × 1.8mm stitch. In trying to practice what I preach, I make samples to determine the size and quality of the stitches I will use for the project.

✦ TIPS FOR SUCCESSFUL BLANKET-STITCHED APPLIQUÉ

Match your bobbin color to the top thread if possible. Libby Lehman's Bottom Line thread is great for this! It is designed for use in bobbins and comes in all colors (see Resources on page 92).

Use a layer of Ricky Tims' Stable Stuff (a polyester stabilizer that you can tear away—or not) under the appliqué. This will stabilize the fabric and help you create smooth and beautiful stitches.

If your machine has the needle-down position, use it! It is very difficult to accomplish quality machine-appliqué stitches without having a needle-down function to keep the stitch in place when the presser foot is raised for pivoting. (Hey, if you don't have a needle-down option, maybe that's a good excuse for a new machine, but don't tell anybody I said so—I don't want to get in trouble!) If your machine does not have this feature, manually position the needle in the down position before raising the presser foot.

Begin sewing the appliqué by using a few straight stitches along the edge of the appliqué. I use a straight stitch with a needle position slightly altered (to the right). This works for me because the horizontal movement of the double blanket stitch on my Bernina goes to the left and right of center. If my straight-stitch needle position is altered to the right, then when I switch to the double blanket stitch, the straight stitches are aligned with the forward and back (vertical) stitches . . . and away I go. Please understand that it is not possible to offer pointers on every model and brand of machine. I can only urge you to find the best solutions with your machine by making test samples.

Keep the vertical stitches as close to the right edge of the appliqué as possible when stitching. The stitches should not pierce the appliqué, but should *just touch* the appliqué edge. This is very important for achieving successful results.

Keep the horizontal stitches perpendicular to the straight stitches, even when rounding a curve. Larger curves are fairly easy—you can scooch the fabric and turn it as you sew. However, on tight curves, you will need to do one set of stitches at a time by stopping when the needle is to the right. With the needle down, lift the presser foot by hand (or with a knee lift if your machine has this feature) and pivot slightly to make sure the next stitch will be sewn toward the center of the curve.

The illustration at right shows a sharp outer point, a sharp inner point, and a tight curve. Note the three sets of side stitches at the inner point. Also note how the side stitches on the curve are all perpendicular to the outer edge of the curve.

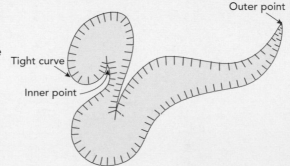

Outer point

Tight curve

Inner point

Stitching an Inside Point

The following instructions relate to how I stitch using the specific features of my particular Bernina sewing machine. Again, the main message is to establish a series of steps that work for your particular situation.

1. Stitch up to the point and stop with the needle down and to the right, having just completed a left, right, left, right sequence; stop stitching. The needle should be down at that inside corner, touching the edge of the appliqué. Reselect the double blanket stitch. This resets the stitch sequence to the beginning, a feature that is important for the next step.

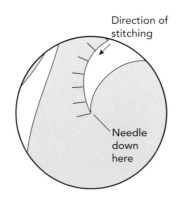

Stitch to the corner; needle to the right.

2. Raise the presser foot and pivot the work because the side stitch will be the first stitch taken. Stitch left, right, left, right, and stop again. These stitches should go onto the appliqué directly at the corner at a perpendicular (right) angle. We are leaving out the forward stitches and backstitches during this corner treatment by reselecting the double blanket stitch.

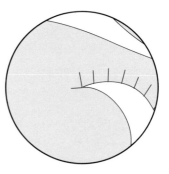

Raise the presser foot, pivot, lower the presser foot, stitch.

3. Reselect the double blanket stitch to start the stitch pattern at the beginning. Lift the presser foot, pivot, and lower the presser foot. Stitch left, right, left, right, and then continue sewing the appliqué.

Lift the presser foot, pivot, lower the foot, stitch.

To review: Once you reach the inside corner (or point), the stitches went left, right, left, right; pivot. Left, right, left, right; pivot. Left, right, left, right; continue. As you can see, restarting the stitch pattern avoided any forward and back stitches.

SEWING THE PIECES TOGETHER

Once the individual pieces are complete (prepared with registration marks, stay stitched, and appliquéd as desired), they are ready to be joined.

Unlike traditional piecing, with this method, you align the stay stitching rather than the raw edges of the fabric. You will not use a traditional ¼" seam allowance. Instead you will use the stay stitching and the special distance you used when you prepared the pieces.

Matching the registration marks is the *single most important step* in the stitching process. If those registration marks start to wander, the pieces *will not go together* cleanly. I find that without pins, I am able to see each registration mark clearly as I sew, and the resulting curved seam is smoother. For this photo sequence, we will use the practice sample from Preparing the Units on page 38.

1. Place the pieces to be joined right sides together. Don't try to align the two edges; the curved edges will usually go in opposite directions. Align only the first ½", so the stay stitching on the top piece is perfectly aligned over the stay stitching on the bottom piece.

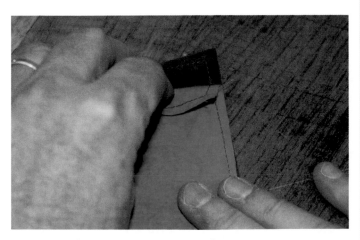

Align the first ½".

2. Sew slightly to the left of the stay stitching, making the distance between the new stitching and the stay stitching equal to *your* special distance—the distance you allowed between the stay stitching and the edge of the freezer-paper template (page 38).

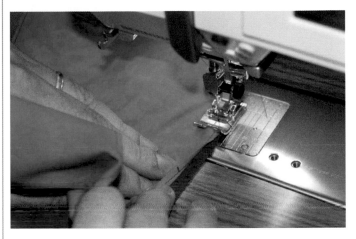

Sew just left of the stay stitching.

3. Continue sewing the seam a little bit at a time, aligning the stay stitching and matching the registration marks as you go. If either the top or bottom piece needs a slight adjustment—that is, tugging or easing—do so as you sew to the next registration mark.

Use your fingers to straighten out the curves, so the stitching line is fairly straight for 2"–3" in front of the needle. These curves tend to be gentle, so "finger tugging" them into place usually is not too difficult. If you continue to align the stay stitching and match the registration marks as you sew, you'll achieve a smooth and gentle curve with no bumps or jags along the seam.

Continue sewing, aligning stay stitching and matching registration marks.

4. Finish the seam and open it to check for any stay stitching that did not get caught in the seam allowance. If the stay stitching shows slightly on the right side of the unit, you may be able to cover it by taking a *slightly* deeper bite into the seam. In some cases, if the seam is secure and the curve looks good, you can carefully pick out the visible stay stitching instead. If neither solution works, you will need to redo the section where the stay stitching shows. Use a seam ripper to remove a portion of the stitching that joins the units, realign the stay stitching and registration marks, and try again.

Visible stay stitching

As you become more comfortable with this technique, you'll soon learn to hold the fabric so the stay stitching remains aligned—and therefore invisible on the joined sections—as you sew.

NO-PINS SET-IN CORNERS

Setting-in straight and curved corners have become two of my favorite techniques. Besides taking pleasure in the process, I enjoy seeing the bewilderment—and then the surprise—when the viewer realizes the seams in the corners have been set-in rather than butted or mitered. The results of this technique are so subtle that I once received complimentary remarks on a judge's score sheet praising my appliqué . . . however, there wasn't any appliqué on that quilt! The curves, corners, and circles featured in that quilt were all pieced.

Most quilters avoid set-in corners because it is easier to construct a design with borders that are butted or mitered. I didn't begin experimenting with set-in corners

until I began dyeing multicolored fabrics. I found that these fabrics lost their beautiful, flowing, blended effect when the border corners had butted or mitered seams.

With set-in corners, I am able to create a continuous color flow at the corners of my quilts. Moreover, when those corners feature intricate quilting designs, I don't have any distracting seams in the quilted areas.

Corner detail of my Convergence quilt, *Bolero*. Notice how the set-in corner allows the fabric motif to flow unbroken around the corner of the quilt. (For a full view of this quilt, see *Ricky Tims' Convergence Quilts*.)

Set-in corners and set-in curved corners both utilize the template-preparation methods (and some of the sewing techniques) outlined in No-Pins Precision Curved Piecing (page 38). This section simply adapts those methods to these particular design elements.

I began by learning to set in square corners. Once I felt comfortable and confident with that technique, I decided to attempt a set-in corner with curves. *Rhapsody in Green* (page 36) has outer borders that were set-in using this method. *Bohemian Rhapsody* (page 9) also features a number of these set-in corners. While this method does require more fabric, I find the results are well worth the sacrifice—especially on a quilt that could become an heirloom.

Once I became confident sewing set-in seams, I started using the technique more and more often, and I think you will too! The exercises on the following pages will help you get started. Be sure to practice sewing both square and curved set-in corners before stitching your Rhapsody quilt.

Preparing Units
for Set-In Square Corners

1. Cut a 12″ square of freezer paper. Use a regular #2 pencil to draw an 8″ square in the upper left corner of the large paper square as shown. Use a different-colored pencil to make registration marks approximately every 1½″ to 2″ along the drawn seam lines.

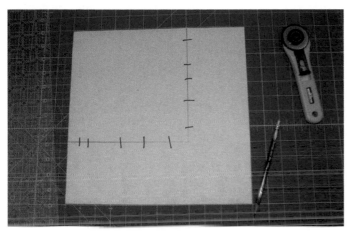

Cut a square, draw a smaller square, and make registration marks.

2. Carefully cut the 8″ square from the larger freezer paper square along the drawn lines. You now have 2 templates: the 8″ square and the larger L shape.

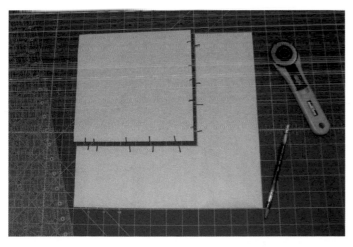

Cut out the smaller square.

3. Iron each template to the *right* side of a different fabric. Rough cut approximately ½″ away on all sides.

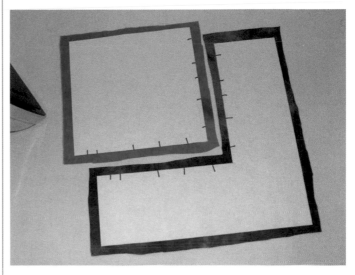

Cut fabrics using the templates.

4. Stay stitch around each template as described in No-Pins Precision Curved Piecing (page 38), trim the seam allowance to a scant ¼″, and extend the registration marks from the templates, marking them in the seam allowance of the fabric.

 Tip

I usually trim the final seam allowance by simply eyeballing it using a rotary cutter.

Trim the seam allowance and add registration marks.

5. Peel away the freezer-paper templates.

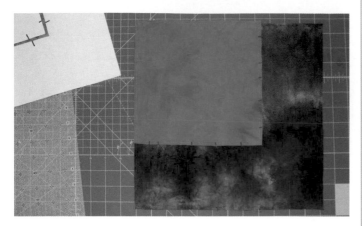

Remove templates.

Setting In a Square Corner

1. Snip the corner of the prepared L piece at a 45° angle as shown, clipping just a hair beyond the stay stitching.

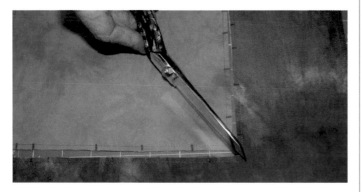

Clip the corner.

2. Position the pieces right sides together as shown. Align the stay stitching and registration marks. Align the snip in the L piece *just inside* the stay stitching in the corner of the square, which is hidden underneath.

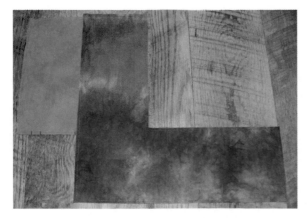

Align pieces right sides together.

3. Fold the lower "leg" of the L back and under, out of the way as shown.

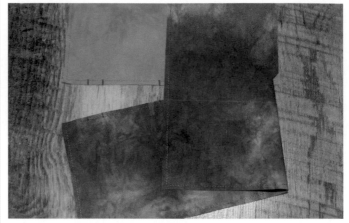

Fold excess fabric back out of the way.

Detail of the alignment at the corner

4. Begin sewing the seam about 2″ from the inside corner as shown, aligning the stay stitching and matching the registration marks. Sew just to the left of the stay stitching, your special distance (see page 38 for details, if needed). The seam should catch one thread of the L fabric right at the corner where it has been snipped. Continue sewing off the edge of the square. There is no need to backstitch.

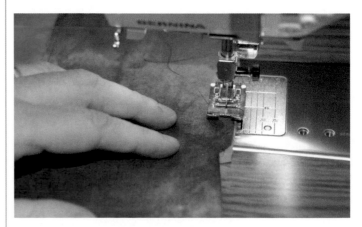

Stitch from 2″ to the edge of the square.

5. Flip the unit over. Begin sewing where the previous stitching started and complete the seam you started in Step 4. Remember to match the registration marks and align the stay stitching.

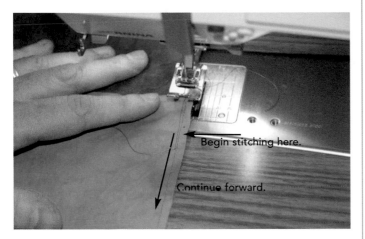

Begin stitching here.

Continue forward.

Finish stitching the seam from the other side.

6. Open the unstitched leg of the L and position it right sides together with the square as shown. Align the stay stitching and match registration marks. Begin sewing at the edge of the square at the inside corner (again, no need to backstitch) and onto the L piece, catching one thread of the L fabric at the snip. Stitch to the end, open the unit, and press. I usually press the seams toward the border, but your project may dictate pressing the opposite way.

Begin sewing at the inside corner.

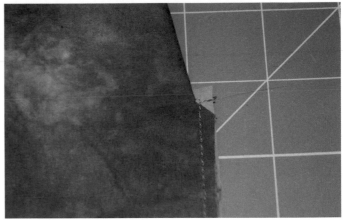

A detail of the corner positioned correctly and ready to be sewn

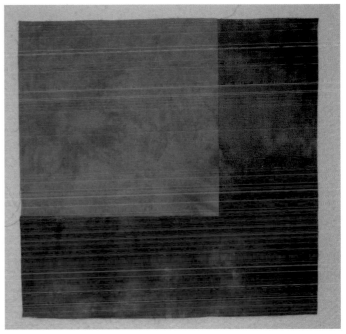

The finished set-in corner

Preparing Units
for Set-In Curved Corners

The steps I take to set in curved corners are identical to those used to set in straight corners. The only difference is how I manipulate the curved seam as I sew. The corner design in a curved corner tapers to a point. When you create a curved corner, make sure this point is reasonable —that it is possible to sew! If the corner tapers too deeply, the closer you get to the corner, the smaller the seam allowance you'll have to work with. As always, when in doubt, make a sample and test the design first before using it in your quilt.

Below are two curved-corner designs. The design on the left is a good example of a gently tapered point—very doable. The example on the right tapers quickly and deeply to a very sharp and narrow point. It may not be impossible to sew, but it would certainly be more difficult and likely require practice. If it were my quilt, I would simply alter the taper to be more reasonable for piecing.

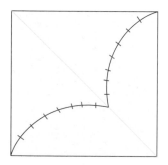

This is an example
of a reasonable taper.

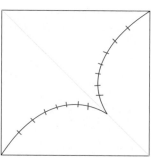

Avoid deep tapers
such as this one.

1. Cut an 18″ square of freezer paper and fold it along one diagonal, shiny side in.

Use a regular #2 pencil to draw a floating curved line from the diagonal fold to the short side of the triangle as shown. Use a different-colored pencil to add registration marks along the drawn seam lines.

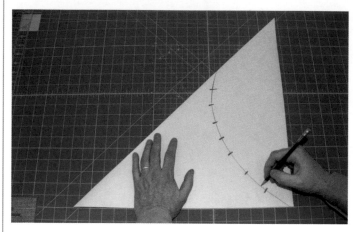

Cut and fold freezer paper. Draw a
curved line and registration marks.

2. Open the paper and refold it, dull (paper) side in. Refer to Creating the Skeleton (page 24) as needed and make a ghost tracing to transfer the drawing onto the other side of the diagonal fold. Transfer the registration marks as well.

Transfer the drawing.

3. Open the paper and darken both the design and the registration marks. Carefully cut the smaller shape from the larger, 18″ freezer-paper square along the lines. You will now have 2 templates: a curved L piece and a "square" with 2 tapered edges.

Darken the lines and cut apart.

4. Iron the tapered square shiny side down to the right side of one fabric. Iron the tapered "L" shiny side down to a different fabric. Rough cut the fabric approximately ½″ all the way around the template.

Iron onto fabric and cut out.

5. Stay stitch around each template using your special distance as described in No-Pins Precision Curved Piecing (page 38). Trim the seam allowance to a scant ¼″ and extend the registration marks from the templates to the fabric.

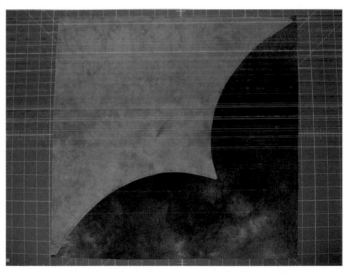

Stay stitch, trim, and add registration marks.

6. Peel away the freezer-paper templates and lay out the pieces right side up, just as they will appear when sewn together.

Remove freezer paper and place pieces right side up.

Setting-In a Curved Corner

1. Snip the corner of the prepared curved L piece at a 45° angle as shown, clipping just a hair beyond the stay stitching.

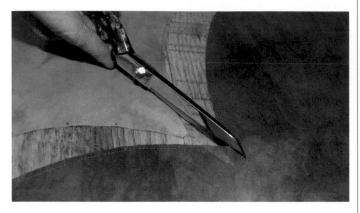

Clip the corner.

2. Position the pieces right sides together as shown. Align the snip in the curved L piece *just inside* the stay stitching on the tip of the tapered square.

Position the pieces.

3. Fold the lower "leg" of the curved L back and under, out of the way as shown.

Fold out of the way.

4. Position the unit under the presser foot as shown with the bulk of the curved L piece out of the way. Begin sewing about 1″ from the corner and stitch the pieces together up to the corner and off the edge, aligning the stay stitching and matching the registration marks. Stitch across the snip, catching one thread of the curved L fabric.

Stitch toward the corner across the snip and catch one thread of curved L fabric.

5. Flip the unit over. Begin sewing where the previous stitching started and complete the seam you started in Step 4. Straighten the curves by gently tugging them as you sew the seam. Keep the stay stitching aligned and match registration marks as you sew.

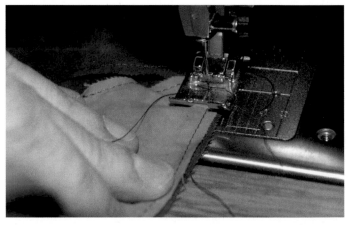

Flip unit over and begin sewing at previous stitching.

6. To sew the other side of the L, position the unit under the presser foot so that you will begin sewing at the inside corner. Begin at the edge and sew into the snipped area, catching one thread of the fabric at the snip. Continue sewing the seam, aligning stay stitching and registration marks. Sew just to the left of the stay stitching, keeping as close as possible. Open the unit and press. I generally press the seams toward the border, but your project may dictate pressing the opposite way.

The finished cut in tapered corner

 **Tip**

As you might imagine, the inside point is *very* fragile. Do not tug or pull on that area of the unit. Even the weight of the fabric can cause the point to fray, so take extra care when handling and positioning these units.

NO-PINS SET-IN CIRCLES

Most quilters have experience sewing traditional curved seams, such as those found in the Drunkard's Path block and the like. Those designs feature a quarter-circle sewn into a curved background piece.

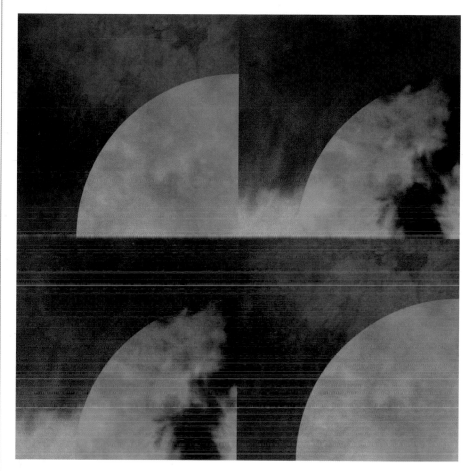

Four *Drunkard's Path* blocks

Sewing a circle into a hole somehow seems mysterious, but it is really just a continuation of the Drunkard's Path. I assure you it isn't overly difficult. As a matter of fact, anytime I have a design that calls for a circle (6″ or larger), I use the following method for setting in circles. Like set-in corners, set-in circles require the same template preparation and some of the sewing techniques outlined in No-Pins Precision Curved Piecing (page 64), as well as Setting-In a Curved Corner (page 38). This section simply adapts those methods to circles.

Naturally, if a circle is to be set in, it needs something to be set *into*—a hole! That means that if the circle is going to be part of your quilt, you'll need to cut a hole in your quilt top. Sound scary? Well, as always, practicing on a sample is the best way to become comfortable with this technique. As I said before, you'll soon discover it isn't all that difficult. The following directions will allow you to learn this valuable skill before cutting a hole in your quilt. Be sure to practice sewing set-in circles before stitching on your Rhapsody quilt.

Preparing Units for Set In Circles

1. Cut an 18″ square from freezer paper. Use a regular #2 pencil to trace a dinner-plate-size circle on the dull (paper) side of the freezer-paper square.

2. Use a different-colored pencil to draw three registration marks *very* close together at the 9 o'clock position on the drawn circle, as shown. Draw 2 registration marks *very* close together at the 3 o'clock position. On the remainder of the circle, draw a series of single registration marks spaced approximately 1½″ to 2″ apart. Make these marks solid and strong, crossing the circle by at least ¼″ inside and out.

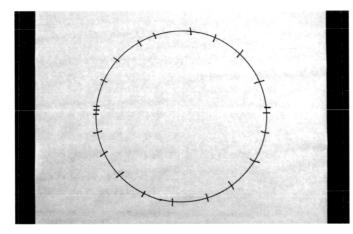

Draw a circle and add registration marks.

3. Carefully cut the circle shape from the freezer-paper square. You will now have 2 templates: a circle and a "square donut."

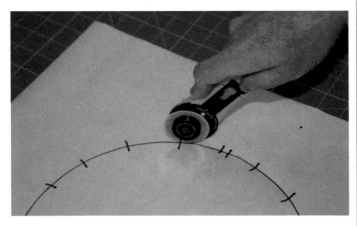

Cut out the circle.

4. Iron each template to the right side of a different fabric.

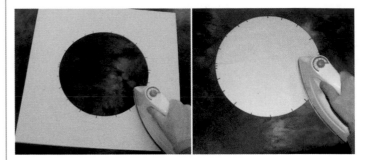

Iron each template onto fabric.

5. Stay stitch around the circle of each template as described in No-Pins Precision Curved Piecing (page 38). This may feel a bit odd on the square donut piece, because you are stitching on the inside of a curve. Extend the registration marks from the templates, marking them on the fabric.

Stay stitch around the template.

6. Cut the pieces from the fabric, leaving a scant ¼″ seam allowance all around, and peel away the freezer-paper templates.

Trim seam and remove the freezer paper.

Sewing the Circle in the Hole

1. Place the prepared square donut right side up with the three closely spaced registration marks in the nine o'clock (left) position. Position the circle in place, right side up, over the hole, matching the three registration marks at nine o'clock.

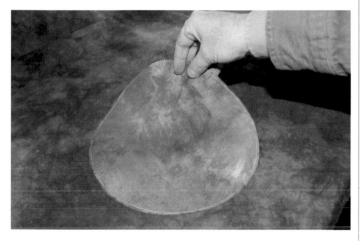

Position the circle, matching the registration marks.

2. Imagine that the 3 registration marks are a hinge, and swing the circle open to the left, keeping the 3 registration marks matched. The circle and square donut are right sides together. (In other words, the circle is now wrong side up to the left of the hole with the registration marks face to face on top of each other.)

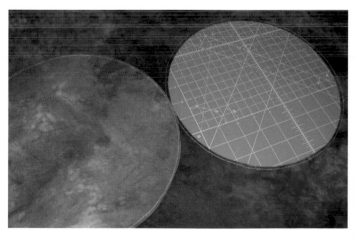

Swing the circle open.

3. Pinch the three registration marks at the "hinge" and lift up. The circle and donut fabrics will hang down while the three registration marks are held between your fingers.

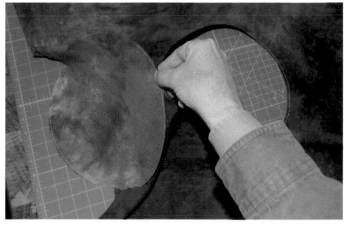

Lift up.

4. Place the unit under the presser foot of your sewing machine, with the 3 registration marks matched and the stay stitching aligned. Because you are working with opposing curves, you'll only be able to work with about 1″ at a time.

5. Begin sewing just to the left of the stay stitching, straightening the curves by tugging them slightly as you sew. Keep the fabrics tugged straight right in front of the needle and work just a few stitches at a time. If your machine has a needle-down feature, this is the time to use it. The needle-down position acts as a third hand— very helpful when the other two are occupied with straightening the curve!

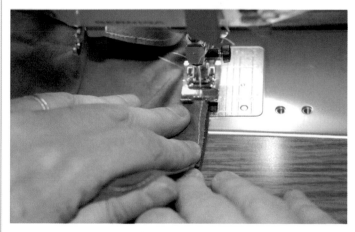

Stitch.

6. Continue to sew slowly around the circle, matching registration marks exactly and keeping your sewing stitches just a fraction to the left of the stay stitching. Look ahead to the next registration mark to determine if you need to tug or ease either piece for the marks to match.

7. Eventually you'll notice that you need to pull the fabric circle through the hole to complete the stitching. It will make perfect sense when it happens: pull it through and finish sewing the seam. If you have sewn just to the left of the stay stitching and matched the registration marks along the way, the circle will fit the hole perfectly.

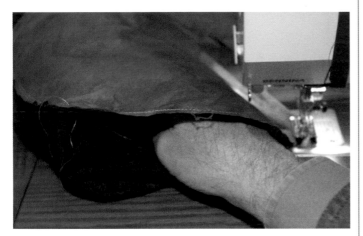

Pull the fabric circle through the hole and finish stitching.

8. Press the seams toward the circle to add a bit of dimension to the circle for an appliquéd appearance.

The completed set-in circle

COMBINING CURVED PIECING AND SET-IN CORNERS

More than likely, your Rhapsody quilt will have a completely set-in unit such as the center portion of *Bohemian Rhapsody* (page 9). Once you have mastered the no-pins techniques (Precision Curved Piecing and Set-In Corners and Circles), you can easily set in a unit that has curved piecing and set-in corners. Simply keep the registration marks matched and make sure that you carefully set in each corner as you go. Be very sure to position the unit correctly. Your randomly spaced registration marks will help you align it properly if and when you become confused as to exactly how to position the unit in place.

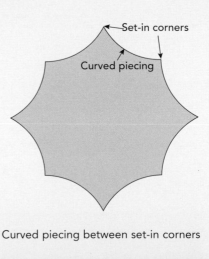

Curved piecing between set-in corners

Detail of *Bohemian Rhapsody* center, showing an entirely set-in unit with both curved piecing and set-in corners

TIPS FOR QUILTING YOUR RHAPSODY QUILT

Just as with appliqué, create the quilting designs directly on the freezer paper templates (dull side). Sketch lightly so you can erase. If you are hesitant to use your templates, trace the template onto another piece of paper—I use freezer paper—and design on the duplicate. Remember: You want the quilting designs to emulate the shape of the template and fit perfectly into the space.

Rhapsody quilts almost beg for traditional quilting—feathered vines and wreaths, crosshatching, cables, and so on. Overall quilting designs that cross over appliqués and seams don't really enhance these quilts. And, because the pieced sections are so unique in shape, it is usually difficult to find a pre-made, commercial quilting pattern or template that fits perfectly.

There are many ways to get around this. For example, you can learn to draw your own quilting patterns. These pages don't cover that aspect of quiltmaking—that's not what this book is about, and besides, it's topic enough for its own book! However, yours truly has a DVD called *Grand Finale: Fine Machine Quilting and Finishing Techniques*, which deals with all aspects of finishing a quilt, including creating your own quilting designs. Check out Resources (page 92) for more information. Meantime, here are some examples to get you started.

The quilting in *Rhapsody in Green* is totally freehand. None of these feathers were marked in advance and no two are alike.

Dad's Lone Star has an unusual orange area with an original quilting design I created just for that space.

The border quilting on *Bohemian Rhapsody* is an original design.
Notice how the feathers follow the curve of the template.

Rhapsody Hearts pattern
¼ of block

Center

DESIGNS TO TRY

Although I strongly encourage you to try the exciting process of creating your own Rhapsody designs, here's a little bonus for those of you who prefer a quick start and want to jump right in: five ready-to-go designs to choose from. Simply enlarge the pattern of your choice to the desired size as described in Creating a Full-Size Pattern (page 30), design and add appliqué, and you are good to go. I've included a diagram of the full skeleton to give you a preview.

SKELETON 1

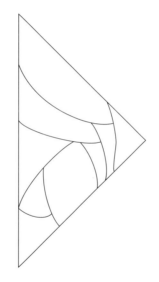

SKELETON 2

SKELETON 3

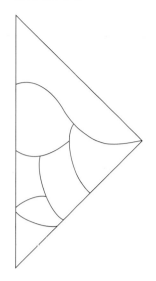
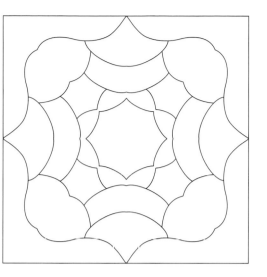

SKELETON 4

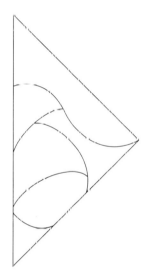
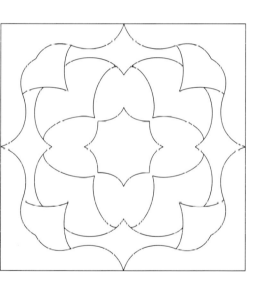

SKELETON 5

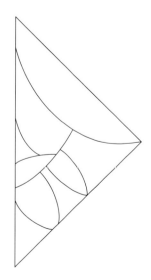

GALLERY
OF QUILTS

Here is a collection of Rhapsody quilts made by quilters who have attended my Rhapsody classes and seminars. In addition to a photo of the complete quilt, each page includes a statement from the artist and a close-up to show you a special element. I think you'll agree that the quilts—and the variety—are amazing. Enjoy the show and revel in the inspiration. The message is simple if they can do it, so can you!

BRIGHT EXPECTATIONS, 72″ × 72″
Completed in 2005, Maureen Squires Capshew, Lanesville, IN.

I went to Ricky's lecture in Paducah in April 2005 and truly couldn't sleep that night because of the visions of Rhapsody quilts in my head! Upon returning home, I began my project with gusto. I had purchased a piece of hand-painted fabric from Laura Wasilowski (www.artfabrik.com) several years before that was so beautiful I hadn't been able to cut into it. Finally, I had the courage. I played with my paper squares until I was happy with my design, and tried my best to follow Ricky's directions for piecing and appliqué. Once I finally finished the top, I went on to my favorite part, the quilting. I thought I was being quite brave to choose a solid black for the backing; with lots of bobbin changes I was able to successfully show the design in thread on the reverse.

his piece was started in a workshop with Ricky Tims in January 2006 when he came to our guild to present his Rhapsody Quilts workshop. My design developed fairly quickly, as did the making of the quilt top. The piece sat for some time while I contemplated how to quilt it. Once I decided on a name for the piece, the quilting designs began to flow. Arabesque relates to the decorative melodies of classical music. My ornate quilting designs incorporate curves, swirls, and intricate geometric patterns. The fabrics are all commercial batiks; the appliqué and quilting were done with cotton and polyester threads, and the bobbin quilting with Ricky Tims' Razzle Dazzle thread from Superior Threads.

ARABESQUE, 42″ × 42″
Completed in 2006, Daphne Greig, North Saanich, BC, Canada.

AUTUMN RHAPSODY, 18″ × 18″
Completed in 2006, Leigh Elking, Scottsdale, AZ.

When Ricky stated in his seminar that Rhapsody quilts didn't lend themselves to miniatures, my immediate thought was, why not? It wouldn't be easy—techniques would have to change—but it's possible!

I found it amusing that every section in my initial drawings was changed by the time I had finished the final quilt! The drawing and revising process (full-size design) took a month before I had the repeating shapes that I liked. Twice I had to reduce my motifs to create enough negative space around the images to showcase them.

A miniature needs to have smaller stitches. I tried several different quilting patterns on my full-size drawings and found that additional designs detracted from the existing motifs. It was challenging to control the stippling between the motifs while maintaining the same size and density. Frequently I had to go back to paper-and-pencil practice before I could continue quilting.

Soaring Rhapsody is the first quilt I designed in a Ricky Tims Rhapsody class taught at the Jinny Beyer seminar in early 2005. As a committed hand-appliquér and quilter, I immediately decided to do this quilt by hand rather than by machine. Because I was away from my extensive stash, the colors were chosen from a group of hand-dyed fabrics purchased from Ricky at the class. The name Soaring Rhapsody references the blue and green design elements that resemble birds in flight.

As with other quilts I've designed, the quilt is very colorful. The size of the center (approximately 35″) was dictated by the largest pieces of fabric I purchased. The dark border, for a stained-glass look around each main appliqué section, was added to the design to ensure sufficient contrast between the design elements and the background. The outer border of the quilt was designed and added after the center section of the quilt was completed.

SOARING RHAPSODY, 45″ × 45″,
Completed in 2006, Charlotte McRanie, Marietta, GA.

PERSEVERANCE, 62˝ × 62˝
Completed in 2007, Debbie Denton, Tulsa, OK.

My first love is hand appliqué; it is so forgiving and portable. I met Ricky Tims at our Oklahoma State Quilting Retreat in the fall of 2000, and I haven't been back inside the traditional box since. *Perseverance* was designed while attending Ricky's Rocky Mountain Quilt Retreat 2002. Four years later, it has been redesigned, sewn, unsewn, cried over, bled upon, and finally finished. The process and techniques I learned along the way were well worth the journey.

his little quilt was the product of a Rhapsody Quilt class presented in Victoria, British Columbia. Ricky's parting advice was, "Use lots of appliqué," so the pieces were designed to fill in most of the spaces.

We live near the Pacific Ocean and during walks along the beach, I have often been enthralled by the colors and patterns of seaweed tossed about in the waves. I tried to imitate the shapes and colors of seaweed in my pattern, which inspired the name *Seaweed Kaleidoscope*. Despite my moderate level of sewing experience, I found this project an interesting challenge and would highly recommend it to even more experienced quilters.

SEAWEED KALEIDOSCOPE, 40″ × 40″
Completed in 2006, Darlene Dressler, North Saanich, BC, Canada.

LA VETA FIESTA, 58˝ × 58˝
Completed in 2005, Marylee Drake, Auburn, CA.

L a Veta Fiesta was conceived and designed at the first La Veta Quilt Retreat in May 2005. I was drawn to Ricky's bold and bright hand-dyed fabrics that reminded me of a Southwestern fiesta. The Rhapsody concept for quilt design provided an excellent opportunity to use these colorful fabrics.

The design is challenging and presented many learning opportunities along the way. Precision piecing, balanced design, color coordination, machine appliqué, and free-motion quilting, as well as a new technique for binding, worked together to keep me focused on finishing this quilt. I think it is a great quilt.

SPRING RHAPSODY, 49″ × 49″
Completed in 2006, Joy Hegglund, Cofton, BC, Canada

Spring Rhapsody was begun in a workshop with Ricky, in Victoria, BC. When building a quilt, I prefer to start with just a very basic idea and see where it takes me. The Rhapsody technique fit me very well, because it started with a folded piece of paper and a few lines; from there it was exciting to see what developed. Once the overall design was on paper, I saw all the tulips that had appeared. The appliquéd tulips and butterflies brought a feeling of spring to the quilt.

I had a real sense of accomplishment when the top was completed, but the quilting was something that I had to continue thinking about for a while longer. After receiving *Ricky's Grand Finale: Fine Machine Quilting and Finishing Technique DVD* as a gift, I was inspired to make my first attempt at trapunto. From there, the quilting just seemed to flow.

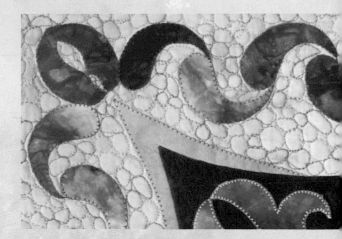

The technique for Rhapsody quilts taught by Ricky Tims is unique. Picking colors is one thing I love and stitching appliqué pieces is another. Starting from the center outward and incorporating sharp points and curved lines into the design was very challenging. Precision curved piecing, using stay stitching and registration marks, joins the pieces perfectly (when done correctly). A variety of free-motion machine quilting gave it the final touches. My best friend, Rosie Metzger, who was very ill, named my quilt *Love's Radiant Energy*.

LOVE'S RADIANT ENERGY, 35″ × 35″
Completed in 2005, Lenny DeGroot, Sidney, BC, Canada.

WINTER DAWN, 53″ × 53″,
Completed in 2004, Leslie Rego, Sun Valley, ID. From a private collection.

I created *Winter Dawn* as a thank-you gift to the Sun Valley Ski Education Foundation. My two sons grew up on the Sun Valley cross-country ski team. It was a wonderful way for teenage boys to have a lot of fun while working very hard. This quilt was auctioned off during the 2004 yearly ski-team fundraiser and is now part of a private collection.

In *Winter Dawn*, I explore the freedoms inherent in machine appliqué. I enjoy drawing big, bold, sweeping designs, which I then cut from hand-dyed fabrics and sew onto background pieces. I used Japanese silk thread to apply the designs because this luxurious filament gives a nice luminescence to the piece. The outer border is one of Ricky Tims' hand-dyed fabrics. I quilted using Japanese silk threads on a long-arm quilting machine.

This quilt was started in Ricky's January 2005 seminar in Victoria, BC. I finished the quilt top during the summer of 2005 and then basted it to quilt while my husband and I traveled the Southwestern United States in our motor home during the fall and winter of 2005.

The opportunity to attend one of Ricky's seminars was a gift and I'm grateful that I had the opportunity. Although I've managed to design a number of quilts, it was quite a struggle for me. It was challenging, but I'm very proud to have met the challenge—it makes this quilt very special to me. The quilt hangs in my studio and I'm gratified that everyone who visits me has commented that it's one of his or her favorites as well.

Another aspect of this quilt that I'm pleased with is the color choices. The fabrics I used contributed immensely to the overall pleasing effect of my Rhapsody—or my "I Did It!"—quilt.

I DID IT!, 39½″ × 39½″
Completed in 2005, Lynne Piper, Saturna Island, BC, Canada.

When I initially drew this design in Ricky's class, I visualized a bud unfolding into the unknown. As the quilt top grew, the design seemed to change, thus the title *Evolving Matter*. The top was finished quickly, even with the deeply inset seams. It is appliquéd with two strands of rayon embroidery thread through the machine needle. A year later, I finally decided on the free-motion quilting style, incorporating my very first feathers.

The flowing lines of this quilt represent a departure from my usual work, because I am a traditional quilter with a strong love of country style. I learned to just go with the flow when designing and I really enjoyed drawing the appliqué shapes. I think the curves are well worth the extra work.

EVOLVING MATTER, 39″ × 39″
Completed in 2006, Peggy Farries, Sidney, BC, Canada.

NORWEGIAN RHAPSODY, 39″ × 39″
Completed in 2005, Wenche S. Hemphill, Victoria, BC, Canada.

This quilt was started in a class with Ricky in January 2005. I come from Norway originally, and the colors reminded me a bit of the Northern Lights, so the title came naturally.

Working out the design following Ricky's directions was exciting, especially when I saw the four units come together. Figuring out the appliqué designs was lots of fun and I feel they complement the main design. I used my machine's regular blanket stitch (with double thread) to appliqué, as that gave me more control going into V-cuts and around sharp points. I used the same color thread as the appliqué thread to quilt in-the-ditch around the appliqué. The outer border was hand quilted using some of the appliqué designs. I used some of Ricky's fabrics and some batiks.

This quilt is one of many in the Victoria Quilters' Guild's recently published journal.

CELTIC RHAPSODY, 68″ × 68″
Completed in 2005, Sharon Murphy, Seattle, WA.

An Irish heritage, combined with a passion for weaving movement and color together in unique ways—these were the inspiration behind *Celtic Rhapsody*. Appliqué, piecing, and trapunto techniques incorporate Ricky's hand-dyed fabrics. The appliqué is highlighted using a buttonhole stitch.

Celtic Rhapsody's star-like pattern deftly weaves together a series of Celtic knots, leafy vines, and interconnected blocks of color, all of which encircle a Celtic Tree of Life in full flower. The quilt's borders utilize trapunto to create a softer echo of the leaf/vine elements, and its edge is finished with a piped binding.

I took Ricky's Rhapsody design course in December 2004. From this experience, I was stretched to create my own Rhapsody quilt. It was so rewarding to be able to design the pattern, choose my own colors and fabrics, and design the quilting.

As I was designing the quilt, I really didn't have anything in mind, but the tulip motif seemed to appear a few times. The colors I chose are all of my favorites. I really like to work with bright, vibrant colors, and some of the fabrics were Ricky's hand-dyed ones that I had been saving for a special project. The quilt has a spring-like quality with leafy vines that complement the tulip theme. The center is the sun, and the red and yellow appliqué designs are the budding tulips.

TULIP RHAPSODY, 60″ × 60″
Completed in 2006, Ellen Lee, London, ON, Canada.

I have been quilting for about 8 years. I enjoy making different types of quilts, including bargello, landscape, pictorial, and, of course, traditional. I find working with color very exciting. When I had the opportunity to take a workshop with Ricky Tims, I jumped at the chance. This was the first time that I had to design my own pattern. Ricky took us through the design process one step at a time and he even made it fun! It was a wonderful learning experience, and I enjoyed working on the quilt using all the different techniques that Ricky taught us. Most of the quilt was made using Ricky's beautiful hand-dyed fabrics and I used Sulky Blendables thread to sew the appliqués. I will definitely use the design process again.

WILD RHAPSODY IN MOTION, 61˝ × 61˝
Completed in 2005, Judy Southcott, Union, ON, Canada;
machine quilted by Mary Anne Charlton.

INDEX

RESOURCES

For a free catalog of C&T books and products, including Ricky Tims' Convergence Quilts:

C&T Publishing, Inc.
Box 1456
Lafayette, CA 94549
(800) 284–1114
ctinfo@ctpub.com
www.ctpub.com

For quilting supplies:

The Cotton Patch
3405 Hall Lane, Dept. CTB
Lafayette, CA 94549
(800) 835–4418
(925) 283–7883
quiltusa@yahoo.com
www.quiltusa.com

Note: Fabric manufacturers discontinue fabrics regularly. Exact fabrics shown may no longer be available.

For information about batting and Steam-a-Seam2 fusible web:

The Warm Company
(800) 234-WARM
(206) 320-9276
www.warmcompany.com

For information about Libby Lehman's Bottom Line, Ricky Tims' Razzle Dazzle, and other threads:

Superior Threads
(800) 499-1777
www.superiorthreads.com

For information about Ricky's Rhapsody Colorée commercial fabrics:
Red Rooster Fabrics
www.redroosterfabrics.com

For information about:
• Ricky's hand-dyed fabrics
• Ricky Tims' Stable Stuff
• Grand Finale: Fine Machine Quilting and Finished Techniques DVD
• Rhapsody Fantastique: Embroidery Designs

Tims Art Quilt Studio & Gallery
P.O. Box 392
105 Ryvs Avenue
La Veta, CO 81055
(719) 742-3755

ABOUT RICKY

Ricky Tims successfully blends two diverse passions into one very unique and interesting career. Thousands who have heard his music affirm his skills as a pianist, composer, and producer. His success as a quilter is equally significant.

He is known in the international world of quilting as an enthusiastic and encouraging teacher, an award-winning quilter, and a talented and spellbinding speaker. His innovative and entertaining presentations feature live music and humor, combined with scholarly insights and wisdom. His quilts have been displayed worldwide, and are highly regarded as excellent examples of contemporary quilts with traditional appeal. He is currently the co-host of *The Quilt Show*, an Internet-based show for quilters that also features Alex Anderson, C&T Publishing author and former host of HGTV's *Simply Quilts*.

Ricky began designing and making quilts in 1991. In 2002, he was selected as one of The Thirty Most Distinguished Quilters in the World. He maintains an international schedule of teaching and speaking engagements, presents *Ricky Tims' Super Quilt Seminars* in select cities throughout the United States, and holds week-long retreats in La Veta, a tiny mountain town located in south central Colorado. He and life partner, Justin Shults, own Tims Art Quilt Studio and Gallery, a space dedicated to promoting quilting as art.

Ricky is passionate about quilting, and is delighted to share his experience and enthusiasm with quilters of every level of expertise. He is challenged by creativity in all forms, and encourages individuals to cultivate self-expression, reach for the unreachable, and believe in the impossible.

Quilting is a relatively new interest compared to Ricky's lifelong passion for music. He began formal music lessons at the age of three. He is a pianist, conductor, composer, arranger, music producer, and performing artist. Tims' music is neither classical, new age, pop, nor world, and yet it could fall under any of those classifications.

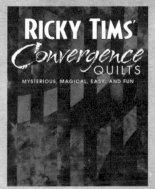

Sacred Age, Ricky's newest recording, was released in January 2006. The album project, featuring solo piano infused with Native American instruments, string orchestra, and vocal orchestrations, was created to suggest the beauty, majesty, and spirit of the Spanish Peaks region of southern Colorado. Tims' music has wide appeal for a diverse audience and has been described as "George Winston meets Carlos Nakai meets Yanni."

Visit Ricky's website: www.rickytims.com.